Parachuting:
The Art of Freefall Relative Work

Flight
for the Joy
of Flying

Fifth Printing (revised) – August 1979
ISBN 0-930438-01-9

©1975
RW Underground Publishing Co.
1656 Beechwood Avenue
Fullerton, Calif. 92635

Library of Congress Catalog Card Number: 75-21405

This book is dedicated to those who would follow Icarus in his self-powered flight but craftily prevent destruction of wings by always falling away from the sun.

Statement of Purpose

Freefall Relative Work

We are a band of brothers, native to the air where we are united in freefall relative work. Our goal is to promote parachuting in general and relative work in particular. RW is a beautiful, exhilarating experience which we like to share with others.

In order to do RW you must relate to others in the air. This relatedness has created a brotherhood of freefall. As brothers we can and should help each other. Because it's OUR sport, we must try to avoid ego-trips, unhealthy politics and hassles. We must promote those aspects of our sport which foster the brotherhood for all.

Good RW promotes itself. RW is where it is today, now. It was non-created. RW just happened and grew. Being non-created, RW is transcendent over acceptance or rejection. Unfettered, it does not ossify into ritual mechanistics and so continues to grow. If directed by a brotherhood of freefallers this growth can strengthen us through unity in numbers. Look how many of us there are today. We are all just beginning. Let's begin together. Do lots of RW.

Pat Works

"Relative Work": (from the French "relatif"): *adj.* relative, relating; *n.* an art practiced by freefall parachutists performed with perfect body and mind control; the movement of the body in the air so that two or more expert relative workers may all fly into various maneuvers such as "star," "snowflake," "wedge" or "bomb-burst funnel"; *syn.* the practice of precision group Skydiving.

In Quest of Perfection...

The Traditions of Freefall Relative Work

1. Our common welfare should come first. Personal satisfaction depends on RW unity: A brotherhood of freefall.
2. There is no central RW authority. Our leaders are trusted servants of the sport; they do not govern.
3. Freefall relative work is democratic and unbiased. The only qualification for membership in the Brotherhood of freefall is a desire to fly for the joy of flying.
4. Each group of RWers has but one primary purpose—to carry the ecstasy and excitement of doing freefall relative work to all parachutists who have enthusiasm for flying.
5. Each RW team or drop zone should be autonomous, except in matters affecting relative work or parachuting as a whole.
6. The Brotherhood of freefall is designed to place principles above personalities and the perfection of flight above all else.
7. The main stem of the Brotherhood is the SCR/SCS awards. The NSCR, 16-man and XX are higher awards.
8. Our relationships with all other parachutists who have yet to join the Brotherhood are based on attraction rather than promotion. The positive results of RW enjoyment, warmth and fellowship emit good vibes which speak louder than any promotion we could possibly do.

Contents

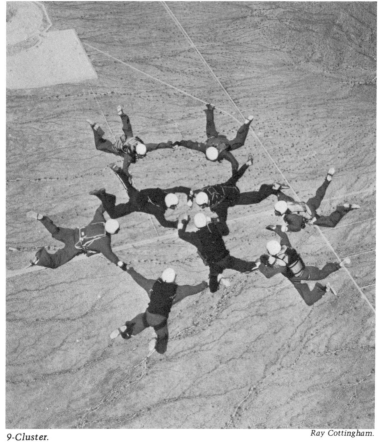

9-Cluster.

Introduction
Art and Speed

Fast-moving precision freefall relative work is an Art along with music, dance, painting and literature. It is a new Art, and one demanding as much theoretical study, natural flair, learning and practice as any of the classical arts.

It is hoped that you will indulge in the art of relative work to a perfection equal to the highest standard of the maneuver you're attempting. Unfortunately there is sloppy and untidy flying everywhere. Unskilled RW flying in traffic or in the formation is one of the major causes of congestion and small stars.

There is a popular misconception that to be good at relative work, one must fly at top speed and fling the body through the air with little or no idea of what is really going on—speed being the all-important element. When you come to realize that speed is essentially a relative property, mastering the art of relative work will be much easier.

Good, fast, precision RW covers a lot more than going fast; it involves a correct relationship between one's mind and body, and the immensely difficult coordination of the senses with physical movements. Speed itself (relative air speed) is less important than perfecting the basic art of relative work flying. If you perfect the basic art of flying first, an increase in speed will come automatically.

Attention to your basic freefall "stable position" will improve your RW. Practice at performing the basic RW maneuvers will result in a more relaxed approach to doing RW which will automatically be followed by improved concentration and being "fast" as the end product.

As the Elder advised Jonathan Livingston Seagull: "Heaven is being perfect...you will begin to touch heaven, Jonathan, in the moment that you touch perfect speed. And that isn't flying a thousand miles an hour, or a million, or flying at the speed of light. Because any number is a limit, and perfection doesn't have limits. Perfect speed, my son, is being there."[1]

Being good...being fast...being there...comes from subconsciously looking ahead a few tenths of a second earlier than you are used to. You will find that time expands from seconds to much longer. This looking ahead will result in greater relaxation, smoother movements, quicker thinking and reaction, and greater appreciation of the exhilarating beauty of skydiving. Your jerky movements will become smooth movements. You'll learn RW. You'll learn your limits of speed.

Conversely, one of the failings of many a would-be flyer is an inability to go fast—ever. He feels he must always "work his way in." But by doing so, he loses air speed, thus lessening his control!

And so this is a book of techniques for the parachutist who would perfect his freefall flying. It is a book of attitude as well. One of control...and abandon. It is meant to be read and studied as you progress toward perfect freedom of expression in flight. It was written with the understanding that parachutists will forever try their wings to achieve the dreams of flight we've all shared.

This book was written because it needed to be written. People who nurture the desire to fly deserve the input of what has gone before. This book relates the truth as we understand it about the art of flying the body. If applied correctly, this art will return to the reader much more than the reading.

[1]Bach, R., Macmillan, 1970.

Chapter I
Theory of Relative Work

How to Fly on Wings of Wind

This chapter will help you to understand flying your body. If you can't grasp it all at this point, reread it after making 15 or 20 jumps in which you've applied some of this theory.

You Can Fly...In the Same Way an Aircraft Does!

Aircraft are either lighter or heavier than air; blimps and balloons on one hand, and airplanes and rockets on the other.

Descending aircraft of both types use gravity as their "power" in place of their engine. Descending aircraft with power "off" and the human body in freefall perform in much the same manner. The rate of descent in feet per second depends on the angle of attack of the body or aircraft on the wind. For both, a high angle of attack results in a glide (track) while a very low angle of attack is a dive.

Fig. 1 Glide (track).

Fig. 2. Vertical Dive.

Both the aircraft and the skydiver's body are controllable in a descent, because both use control surfaces to vary the angle of attack. Both are considered to be flying; just as an airplane in a descent (dive) is not crashing, the skydiver is flying, not falling.

A quote from James Barrie's *Peter Pan:*

One of the high points of the story is when Peter invites Wendy to Never-Never-Land to be storyteller-in-residence:

"Oh dear, I can't. Think of mummy! Besides, I can't fly."

"I'll teach you."

"Oh, how lovely to fly."

"I'll teach you how to jump on the wind's back, and then away we go."

"Oo!" she exclaimed rapturously.

"Wendy, Wendy, when you are sleeping in your silly bed you might be flying about with me saying funny things to the stars."

The wind's back...parlance with constellatory wits ...away we go...suffer, earthbound readers."

...Far out! Lookit...I'm flying!

Flying an Airplane

The aerodynamics of a wing are difficult to understand, tricky to handle. Man has been flying powered aircraft for 70 years, but it's still a difficult art. As parachutists we've been flying our bodies for more than ten years, and it's still just as difficult. This is because in all flight things are often not what they seem to be to our ground-oriented heads. Thus, flying is difficult to learn.

What makes freefall relative work flying so difficult is that the flyer's instincts—his most deeply established habits of mind and body—will tempt him to do exactly the wrong thing. In learning the art of relative work, skills, ideas and habits must be developed where there were none before. In learning the art of RW, much carefully learned behavior and many firmly held ideas must first be forgotten and erased or actually reversed!

It is because of this contrariness to common sense that RW requires "nerve" or full control of the mind. There are many situations in RW when flinching, stiffening up or worrying so as to lose the ability to concentrate will blow the entire jump. And many people who can do RW to the point of entering a star will then blank out and let the formation self-destruct. Or very commonly, beginners will bend over, tense and straighten their legs on entry and bobble, potato-chip or bomb the star. The only recovery from this situation is to RELAX the body and mind. It requires presence of mind, and that isn't easy.

All of this might seem to make learning RW mostly a matter of drill or reflex training, like boxing, judo, fencing, karate, etc. It is. However, there are other routes to learning RW.

It may be that our common sense and our natural reactions mislead us simply because they are working on the basis of wrong ideas in our minds about the body and how it flies. The body is the simplest form of aircraft; it obeys ordinary physical laws. But flying the bold body is new.

RW is done largely with one's imagination. If you have a clear picture of what your body is really doing, can establish its movement realistically, and then orchestrate that movement to the music of the air and relate all that to your brother relative workers, your RW will be effortless and naturally correct.

So if your ideas of "what's what" are correct, you will do RW well. This means we have to take a glance at some Theory of Relative Work.

Theory of Relative Work
The theory of relative work explains how your body is flown without aid of aircraft, open parachute or other devices.

Right now there are thousands of toads who are wishing they could fly. But wishes haven't helped much since Cinderella's Fairy Godmother bounced doing night RW with an elf.

In order to *do* RW, in order to be able to out-fly Jonathan Seagull, to be the Nureyev of the air, or just to get in cleanly without undue mess, you must understand the magic key to doing relative work. The knowledge of it allows you to see what you're doing in technicolor images inside your head. One click unlocks your brain to most of the secrets of the art of flying your body.

In textbooks this magic is confusingly explained under the name of Angle of Attack. Angle of Attack is synonymous with THE theory of RW. If you had only two hours to explain the "how and why" of freefall relative work to a 75-150 jump RW novice, Angle of Attack is what you should explain. According to Wolfgang Langewiesche, "It is almost literally all there is to flight."[2]

Angle of Attack explains vertical dives, the delta, the max-track, mushing, dropping in, flaring, turns, approaches and Z-ing out. It takes the wonder and confusion out of maneuvers like the hand-track or the reverse arch. No RW maneuver can be fully understood without understanding this one thing. While you don't have to know it to do RW, it will help you to learn RW.

You still may be a bit of a clod at swooping; you still may not be able to coordinate your arms, hands, feet, legs and body, but if you understand Angle of Attack, then you'll understand the theory of RW and not be puzzled. You will be able to figure out what you should do. You will be able to analyze your mistakes, and you'll do better each time you try.

Angle of Attack is not an easy thing to understand, however. It is tough to get your gray matter to grasp the initial principles. It is further confused by the fact that your body (fuselage), arms (wings) and feet (rudders) have infinitely variable configurations.

Firstly, angle of attack is NOT the angle which the longitudinal (long part, head to toe) axis of your body makes with the horizon, ground or star; it is NOT the angle at which you aim up or down. Or in other words, it is NOT the "attitude" your body takes to a referent. The distinction is important because you may be head-low and

---

[2]*Stick and Rudder,* McGraw-Hill, 1972, p. 6.

have a very high angle of attack, for example, during a max-track.

Here it is and it's an idea you'll want to ponder and mull over, talk to yourself and draw diagrams, fly around the room with until it finally sinks into your muddled brain: THE ANGLE OF ATTACK IS THE ANGLE AT WHICH THE EFFECTIVE "WING" SURFACES OF YOUR BODY MEET THE AIR.

You technically-oriented, scholarly types should forget Bernoulli's Theorem...it won't help you do RW. Forget about fluid circulation, too. The key fact of freefall relative work is that THE BODY MOVES BY PUSHING THE AIR AWAY...(re-directing it, if you will).

You deflect the air with your arms, torso and legs. It's really important to understand that your entire body must deflect air in order to move. In exerting a downward or sideways force on the air, you scoot forward or turn or whatever—by the famous old theorem known as Newton's law of action and reaction which makes guns recoil, balls bounce, airplanes fly, etc.

Remember that air is heavy stuff. It weighs about two pounds per cubic yard. Thus, if you fling out an arm as your body swoops through this stuff at over 120 mph, you'll get a hefty reaction.

Deflection of air is what makes a relative worker fly. Newton's law says that if the arm pushes the air, the air will return the push. It's as if you were a piece of 4'x8' plywood and jumped out of a Twin Beech (large door) and while falling you wanted to slide over about 500 yards. All you would have to do is angle down the side of the board in the direction in which you wanted to travel and boogie on over.

Eureka!! In the final analysis, a body in controlled freefall is nothing but a variable air deflector. In flight everybody's RW body is curved and contoured to· be as efficient and effective an inclined plane as we can coordinate it to be. (By the way, the PLANE part of airplane is derived from INCLINED PLANE 'cause that's what it is.)

The body as an inclined plane is what we have to

understand. You incline your body so that as it moves through the air, it will meet the air at an angle and shove it aside in somewhat the same way that the inclined plane of a snowplow, in moving forward against the snow, shoves the snow to the side.

And the angle by which it is inclined—the angle at which you meet the air in order to do a specific RW maneuver—is for every skydiver the most important thing in swooping, for THAT is the Angle of Attack. (Drum roll and trumpet fanfare.)

Go fly yourself and check it out.

To demonstrate to yourself the Angle of Attack, go into a track at terminal. Now visualize the Angle of Attack thing. Imagine your entire body acting as a super air deflector. Feel the force of it. Your toes, shins, thighs, torso, arms and neck should each be doing their best to deflect the air.

Hunch your shoulders forward, pull up your chest, suck in your stomach and tuck your chin in. Put your arms to your sides cupping them downward so that your hands and forearms are really pushing the air. Your legs should be straight, with toes pointed or feet placed 90° sideways. Distance between the legs may vary. If you're doing it right you'll feel a very hefty push against everything.

Push! Watch the ground *move* under you. Grab the material on the legs of your jumpsuit. Really get it on. Imagine yourself to be an eagle or a Phantom jet in a dive after prey.

Fig. 3 Two Views of a Max Track

From wingtip to wingtip, your whole body and being should concentrate on achieving maximum deflection of air. You'll feel it when you're there; the speed will exhilarate you.

In this position you have a high Angle of Attack and will cover the most horizontal distance per second.

If you are strong enough you can push too hard and start to stall out into a mush. The drop in speed will be noticeable. In this case you have too high an Angle of Attack. Reduce it and boogie.

Relative Worker, Relative Worker, How Blows the Relative Wind??

Now would you believe an even more realistic picture of what really goes on when we maneuver in freefall? In the demonstration of Angle of Attack, above, we kept things simple. Your angle of attack was rather close to the attitude the longitudinal axis of your body presented to the ground. Or so your head said.

HA! Wrong. Actually the wind wasn't coming straight up from the ground but rather from ahead and below you. Hence the angle of attack cannot be seen simply by looking at the ground or the horizon or the star; **in fact it cannot be seen at all.**

Remember, Angle of Attack is the angle at which the effective wing surfaces of your body meet the air—and we can't see air. That, Bunky, is why RW is an Art. In baseball the batter keeps his eye on the ball he is going to hit. RW is the art of batting the air down with our body as required, but in relative work you can't see the air. Sooo, we often fail to hit it right. We FUBAR up the star and we enter "RW(Attempt)" in our log.

OK, so why not forget it and just keep on trackin' and tryin'? The answer, my friend, is this—if you want to understand RW you must understand the Angle of Attack. Then you have to understand from where, under various conditions of RW maneuvering, comes the air which you are trying to meet and deflect.

When we first started RW, we learned mostly by "monkey see, monkey do" and by asking questions of successful RW'ers on the ground. This mechanical approach at first resulted in several distinct schools of flying around the country. For example, in many cases you can look at a photograph of a star made several years ago and tell in what part of the country it was made by the body configurations of its participants.

Many of these differences in star flying are still with us today. Western jumpers tend to do a more floating kind of RW, using a light, slow-falling base, while in the East or Midwest, the base smokes downward much faster.

This simple difference in the flying speed of the 5-man base makes for vastly different approach techniques and star-flying positions. With a slow-falling star you want to get there quick, grab a "snatch-grip" anywhere between the shoulder and the hand, and then fly the star in a fairly relaxed position. The idea is to keep the base close to the last people out of the plane.

On a smoking base you get there quickly but enter on wrists only and fly in a tight position to keep the star moving fast so the people at the end of the load won't have to slow down to enter.

In either method jumpers are using the Angle of Attack and the Relative Wind to do RW. You could jump with either group by adjusting your Angle of Attack.

What is the "Relative Wind"?
When you ride a motorcycle the wind always blows in your face, right? The same is true of any high speed vehicle. Actually the speed of the vehicle rushing through the air causes the feel of a wind. It's like saying that telephone poles rush by a car. The air doesn't really rush against the motorcycle but the effects are the same as if it did.

This so-called "Relative Wind"—this onrush of air— this "wind of flight" always comes at the jumper from the direction **toward which he is moving.**

Fig. 4. The two bikes moving in opposite directions feel opposite Relative Winds.

While in a dive this Relative Wind comes from ahead and below. If you pull out of a fast vertical dive into a horizontal "swoop," or track, this wind blows from nearly in front of you. While falling stable this wind blows from directly below.

Fig. 5. In a Track. Converting the speed of a dive into a horizontal swoop.

As you do more RW you will practice the side flare and mush and you will develop a sense of your air speed. And importantly, you will develop a feel for the direction of the Relative Wind. You CAN feel it. When an experienced RW'er exits, dives, approaches a star, tracks or flares, he is consciously or unconsciously asking himself all the time, "Where at this moment is the air coming from? And at what angle must my body meet it to do what I want to do?"

Most skydivers will probably deny that they ever think about it. And today most experienced RW'ers don't know the meaning of the words Angle of Attack or Relative Wind. But you can bet your sweet bippy that, subconsciously, most good fliers' minds are on the Relative Wind, although for them it's "feel" rather than deliberate reasoning.

A good relative worker's "feel" for his total body and his almost instinctive ability to handle it right is, on analysis, nothing more than continual awareness of this most important of all flying facts—the Angle of Attack. That is, the angle at which your whole body and its every flying surface meets the Relative Wind.

Think about it. Remember Jonathan Livingston Seagull's words, "As an unlimited idea of freedom, your whole body, from wingtip to wingtip, is nothing more than your thought itself."

Chapter II
Relative Work Maneuvers

Types of RW
There are four types of relative work: terminal, subterminal, momentum and non-momentum. You gotta be good at 'em all.

Non-momentum RW is the kind of RW you learn to do first. You get to within about 30 feet of the dude you want to relate to and are at his level. You stop dead-still and then hand-track over; you have no velocity left over from your descent track.

This type of RW is difficult to do well. Experts at it literally seem to dance on columns of air beneath them. You need to be good at non-momentum RW to enter a squirrelly star or you won't get in. Also, heaven forbid, you might be so fast you go below and the only thing that will get you back up and in is non-momentum RW. On the other hand, if you're going to *be* as fast as you already think you are, then you must be hot at momentum RW, too.

Momentum RW is the kind of RW that builds competition stars. In momentum RW you never stop or slow down; you maintain track-generated velocity and redirect it to enter. You must be very aggressive, and your chances of a wipeout are higher. You generally use the "mush" entry in momentum RW. The "mush" is a high-velocity, sitting-up approach. We'll get into it later.

Relative Fall
Here we want to talk about techniques of performing momentum and non-momentum relative work maneuvers, keeping in mind that the thought behind it all is

Angle of Attack. So all we'll discuss here are maneuvers you do at terminal velocity. Subterminal RW is very specialized because you do not have the flying edge that terminal velocity of 120 mph gives you. The maneuvers are the same, but they must be much more exaggerated and held longer to achieve the same results.

It's unfortunate that students are required to do stable five-second delays before they can progress to longer delays (where they reach terminal velocity and begin to figure it all out.) It's like requiring a student pilot to learn how to do perfect landings and take-offs before you'll teach him to fly.

When you reach terminal, you've reached a relatively constant rate of fall that tends to be uniform with the group you're trying to fly in relation to. Most discrepancies due to body size or mass can be compensated for by jumpsuit or body position.

When many of us think of "falling stable" we usually have as a reference the two positions explained by Russ Gunby[3] as "the basic stable" and the "French Frog".

Fig. 6. Basic Stable.   *Fig. 7. French Frog.*

[3]*Sport Parachuting,* R. Gunby.

These positions are rather rigid: the arms and legs are held down against the Relative Wind. The idea that rigidity is a necessity in the stable freefall position began to dissolve with the advancement of freefall RW which led to the development of the RW Stable.

The principal idea behind the RW Stable position is that it is not a wind-deflecting position at all. The arms and legs are not held out into the wind to act like outriggers on a canoe for the body, but instead they are consciously allowed to blow back behind the body and provide stabilization like the feathers on a badminton bird or an arrow. The arms and legs and head and torso are brought out of relaxation and into play *only* when movement is desired. The achievement of relaxation in this position requires control and awareness in freefall.

Effective Center of Mass.

Fig. 8. RW Stable.

All three positions are stable. They vary only in their rate of vertical fall: the RW Stable being the fastest, the Basic Stable being the slowest. The advantage of the RW Stable is its higher rate of "sink" and its stability. This stability is due to a low center of gravity, or effective center of mass. Style-oriented RW'ers lean to the style "tuck" to achieve this same rate of vertical descent. However, for *most* people the style tuck is too unstable in the rough air around a star, where the RW Stable is preferred.

Effective Center of Mass.

Fig. 9. Style Tuck.

When you fall at terminal velocity with a group, your body size or mass may give you a flying advantage or disadvantage over your fellow jumpers. Nevertheless, whatever your size/mass ratio you'll still use the same basic techniques as everybody else. Since your skrawny or rock-like body is a *constant* to you, you'll naturally adjust your body configurations to keep your rate of vertical fall relative to your co-workers. This self-adjustment is probably the basis for the concept of "relative work".

We want to talk about maneuver techniques, so don't let the relative fall thing lead you astray. If you're tall and skinny you have a larger effective "wing" area to use in deflecting the Relative Wind. If you're short and stocky you'll have rather less effective wing area to use. Importantly, although one "floats" while the other "sinks" they both use Angle of Attack to move; and if they are good at it their body size doesn't matter.

Relative Work Maneuvers

You'll use many different modes of motion in RW. There are different modes of moving for specific situations—some are obvious, some are fancy. Consider dives alone: a skydiver may descend in a vertical dive, a vertical no-lift dive, or a delta.

All together I figure there are five major modes of movement: dives, glides, braking, RW turns, and recovery maneuvers.

Fig. 10. DELTA—Body has high Angle of Attack and develops considerable lift resulting in horizontal movement.

Fig. 11. VERTICAL DIVE —Body points straight down but flight path is not straight down. Body has some Angle of Attack, some lift.

Fig. 12. NO-LIFT DIVE — Body has no Angle of Attack, no lift. Body is slightly inverted. Flight path is straight down.

The Dives

As noted at the beginning of this chapter, all momentum RW approaches start from a dive and its resulting velocity.

The Delta is the most common dive. In a Delta your arms are back alongside your body and a little bit away from it; your legs are slightly separated and your toes are pointed. Your Angle of Attack is moderately high, resulting in a large deflection of the Relative Wind which is coming from below and slightly ahead of you. The Delta gives a medium horizontal speed and a high descent speed. This dive has some "feel" to it since the Angle of Attack requires some muscle pressure from your whole body.

A word about muscle pressure: as a general rule, relaxed to moderate muscle tension gives you the best control in most maneuvers. Use high muscle tension only when you aren't performing a maneuver with enough speed to get good results.

In the Vertical Dive your body points down. The normal configuration of the body in this position produces some lift. The flight path is not straight down, but forward and down because the body has a slight Angle of Attack. The Relative Wind will come from the direction of movement, or from below and just ahead.

The difference between the Vertical Dive and the No-lift Dive is a changed body position which cancels all lift so that the body seems to "fall" out of the sky. There is no angle of attack. There is no lift. The Relative Wind comes from directly below. You are going downward and fast!

To enter a No-lift Dive start from a Vertical Dive, tuck your chin in and roll your shoulders forward as you bend at the waist. You'll feel your body suddenly fall into the burble created by your head and shoulders. You'll be looking back and up. The position feels distinctly inverted. If you feel the wind hitting the backs of your legs you're a bit too inverted.

In making a transition from a stable position to a no-lift dive, you go from a 90° Angle of Attack (no deflection, high resistance to the Relative Wind) to a 0° Angle of Attack (no deflection, minimum resistance to the Relative Wind), resulting in a speed increase from about 120 MPH to over 200 MPH. That's an increase of about 100%. It is redirection of this dive or track-generated velocity that allows us to do **momentum** RW.

However, the conversion of vertical dive-speed into horizontal approach-speed dramatically changes the direction of the Relative Wind, requiring suitable compensations in Angle of Attack if we are to maneuver well. This conversion is called a "Swoop" and it usually results in a low-angle or level approach on the star. There are other momentum RW approaches which work as well or better; the 45° straight-in and the high approach, but we'll discuss those in the chapter on approaches.

There comes a time in any vertical dive when you must arch out of your high-speed descent and cover the horizontal distance to the star.

This change of direction produces a noticeably increased G-load on your body and a dramatic sensation or "rush." At the same time your body muscles come out of inactivity into a wrenching airstream. The "Swoop" is an appropriate name for the transition from dive to track.

The history of the Swoop is lost in the ozone. We do know that its invention came sometime after Stephan and Joseph Montgolfier made man's first ascent in 1783 in a hot-air balloon. Fable tells us that it was invented by the famed C. G. Godfrog.

THE SWOOP: ITS INVENTION
The Fable of The Godfrogs

ONCE UPON A HAPPEN THERE WAS THIS FROG...Carlos Gene Godfrog by name. "C.G." (as his friends called him) was a clumsy green tree-frog by trade. "C.G." was black-balled by the Tree-Frog Union for "chronic falling out of trees."

Falling out of trees not only hurt C.G.'s body, it hurt his big frog ego, too. Since smarting from a bruised ego is an intellectual process, C.G. was able to figure out a solution to the problem.

It came to him one day whilst he was drowning his Sorrow at the local sleazy Frog Pond. The ravaged Sorrow broke loose to gasp out, "Arrrgh-sputter-SWOOP-gasp-HELP!"

"Eureka!" chortled C.G. as he danced down the nearest yellow brick road to the closest tree. He climbed to the top and began with a slow front loop followed by crushing impact with the ground... C.G. had struck upon the concept of the swoop!

Some 287 tries later he was a mottled red, green and blue, but he doggedly lept on. (Frog watchers take note: this Paisley patterned bruise is the sure sign of the novice God-frog.) Finally his patience was rewarded. Carlos Gene God-frog had perfected the SWOOP!

It happened on the day after Shrove Wednesday in the vacant lot behind Farmer Nasty's barn. From a Dutch Elm (DE-1) from 60 feet, he made a 3-second stable delay and basic spread Swoop impact. Carlos' mastery of his mind and his fear of further damage to his body had given him the internal fortitude to develop a panic flare-arch-roll-your-shoulders forward-and-scream-with-eyes-and-mouth-wide-open technique seldom matched today.

Yes, from these clumsy beginnings, Carlos Gene shot forth into national prominence. Not letting the fame, fortune and bright lights go to his battered head, he modestly bought a yacht, two Twin Beeches, a chopper, a stereo, a van, had his hair processed and a new red, white and blue frogskin suit made.

Shortly thereafter, the Tree-Frog Union arrested, tried, convicted, hung, shot and stomped poor Carlos Gene God-frog for the crime of not being green. He was posthumously elevated to the level of deity of the Neo-American Church where his techniques have been taught in a sanctuary located between 3.5 and 12.5 thousand feet.

Today, as you drive down any street, you may notice very flat, spread-out frogs lying by the roadside. These frogs all have the characteristic steamroller-look markings. DO NOT disturb these frogs. They are novice Swoopers, disciple Godfrogs who are undergoing a strict fasting and rest period before attempting their next swoop. They spread themselves out on the roadside to collect energy from the sun and warmth from the asphalt. So deep is their trance they can seldom be aroused except by screaming the sacred mantra "Pull your reserve, for god's sake!"

Glides

In its least efficient form, the track is simply a delta...medium horizontal speed and a fairly high descent speed. However, the objective of the track is different, the configuration is different, and the result is different. In a track, your arms are back, your legs are slightly separated and your toes are pointed...just as in a delta. But your shoulders are rolled forward, your waist is bent slightly and your arms press down with vigor on the Relative Wind.

This results in a high Angle of Attack that produces a large deflection of the Relative Wind which is coming from below and ahead of you. It's similar to a ski-jumper's position with good horizontal speed and a high descent speed. The track is a medium glide you use to descend and cover a good bit of horizontal at the same time. It's a glide with a lot of "feel" due to the muscle action required to obtain the high Angle of Attack. Most RW'ers feel the track to be the best method for covering ground...'taint so.

The fastest mode of horizontal RW flying is the max-track. The max-track is a track modified by the jumper to produce greater horizontal speed, or more accurately, the greatest distance of ground covered on the horizontal plane per foot of fall.   See Fig. 3. page 8.

Since your object is to cover the most ground with the least descent, the basic track is modified to produce a much higher Angle of Attack. From the track you roll your upper torso, head, shoulders and upper arms into an airfoil. Your lower arms, thighs, and lower legs must deflect a maximum amount of air. The Relative Wind blows from ahead and below. You do everything you can to cover horizontal distance without losing altitude. Some jumpers grab their jumpsuit leg material to increase the effective size of their Relative Wind deflector.

The difference between a track and a max-track is readily apparent at break-up altitude when everyone separates to dump...those in a max-track will obviously cover more ground than their tracking companions. If you're not physically fatigued after a max-track, you're not doing it right. Compare Fig. 3 to Fig. 5.

The hand track, another glide maneuver, is generally initiated from a stable position. It is the key maneuver of non-momentum relative work. The hand track is probably the "original" RW maneuver because you start from a dead-still stable at level with those you want to relate to, and with no residual velocity left over from your descent track.

From the stable position you bring your forearms and hands down in front of you and hunch your shoulders forward, while at the same time straightening your legs. The angle of attack of your arms, shoulders and legs is very high. The Relative Wind blows from directly below; you use a lot of arm and leg muscles to push down on it. (After a heavy bout of non-momentum RW your pectoral muscles will be sore.)

Fig. 13. Hand Track.

The hand track is used on potato-chipping stars, large-star attempts, after the first maneuver in sequential RW, and in speed-star work whenever traffic or the situation requires it.

The backslide is a kind of reverse track. Use it when your approach is too high or when the formation slides toward you while you are on final approach. When the star is poorly flown or if a person entering the side opposite you floats his side up, the star will rush at you and you can easily get credit for bombing it. When you get rushed by a star you can either turn away and try again, or backslide.

Fig. 14. Backslide.

To perform the backslide, throw your arms out above your head at a high angle. The back is arched slightly and the feet are tucked up out of the way on your ass. Don't let your knees get very far apart. The arms and torso are adjusted to obtain the required rate of backslide versus descent. The rate of descent is high since the legs aren't in use. The angle of attack is controlled by the arms. The Relative Wind comes from below and behind.

If a backslide is entered too abruptly without an adequate arch, a backloop results. This maneuver is called "Z-ing out" and is not allowed, so be careful.

If you're level with the star and it wantonly "attacks" you, the backslide won't help because you'll have a higher descent rate than the star. In other words, the backslide is used generally with a high approach and is considered an advanced maneuver. The backslide differs from a flare in configuration and in objective.

On the other hand, all is not lost if a star at your level "attacks" you while on final approach. You can still get out of its way without losing precious altitude...by flying backwards!

Flying backwards? Yep! The ability to fly backwards often means the difference between getting into a star that is "rushing" you or having to turn and run. You'll have set up your approach only to find that the star is sliding toward you at a rate which exceeds your ability to maintain the proper approach angle for a good entry. If you get too high on the oncoming star, it becomes crashingly easy to end up on someone's back.

Flying backwards enables you to maintain your optimum approach angle. You fly backwards as you descend into your onrushing slot. Obviously this is an advanced relative work maneuver.

Sometimes flying backwards is simply a controlled backslide. For example, you find yourself too high and at the same time too close to the formation to enter cleanly. The formation seems to be eating you up, so to speak. It may even fly underneath you. You can backslide out of the way, and still get in.

Fast sequential RW, such as international four-man, requires that the point man be able to fly backwards. On the Murphy Star, the Diamond and the Caterpillar, for example, a precision point man will backloop, do his 180° turn, and fly backwards toward an area in the center of his teammates designated as the contact area. This maneuver produces the fastest time.

Also, it is impossible to do some of the more advanced alternate and sequential maneuvers, such as the Tri-Bi-Pole in Fig. 15, without having a couple of flyers who can fly in reverse with precision.

Learn to fly backwards, but don't try to learn on a big load. It costs everyone else too much money if your hot-shot RW trick doesn't quite work the first time you try it.

Fig. 15. The Tri-Bipole.

Braking

When you smoke down to an RW maneuver your closing speed is as high as 80-100 MPH. This speed may be all horizontal or a combination of vertical and horizontal, i.e. at an angle. It could also be all vertical. Whichever it is, you have to be able to slow down enough to dock and enter.

You're going a lot faster than the star is because you've reduced your angle of attack and reduced the effective area of your body by presenting less of it to the Relative Wind.

If you used a vertical dive approach and arched out to swoop in on the star from about its level, then your speed has a high horizontal component and the Relative Wind is blowing from ahead of you and slightly below. If you took a 45° dive at the star, the Relative Wind will come from ahead and below. If you did a max-track over to the area directly above the star and then dove down to it in a no-lift dive, the Relative Wind comes from directly below. If you can't feel the real direction of the Relative Wind your braking maneuver, or flare, can't be fully effective and you're wasting time and motion.

Depending on your approach technique, your flare will stop you at wrists or some distance out. In theory, you should dive as long and as fast as you can, brake as hard as you can at the latest possible instant and then smile and enter. That's theory. That's the way you drive a race car, too—go as fast as you can up to a curve, delay braking as long as possible to still be able to make the turn, and press on to victory.

However, you're no race car and the star you're working on is not an inanimate turn. The RW formation you're burning in on is made up of your living friends who may be bouncing around in the star causing it to move about the sky. Imagine how a race driver would feel if the approaching corner moved sideways *and* up and down as he approached it! Imagine how your friends would feel if you used the racing driver approach and muffed it! Imagine how you would feel if you wrecked the star!

Since the star does move, a cool approach is necessary. Leave some flare-power to take care of emergencies. So, while your flare may start out as a body-wrenching, balls-out thriller, you must maintain reserve and FULL control as you near the star. You must know from whence blows the Relative Wind, as mentioned earlier, and you must adjust your flare to the Relative Wind.

The basic flare is a reversed basic stable position, a backward student arch otherwise known as a reverse arch. Chances are that what you believe to be your full-on maximum flare isn't much more than a flat basic stable. Think about it...if you can't see your hands and feet in a flare and if it doesn't hurt, then it's not a full flare, so there.

This "full flare" differs from a "recovery" maneuver in that you are entering from above in a braking flare, while a "recovery" is designed to recover altitude before entering.

To perform a full flare, start from a basic stable and reverse your arch until you can see your hands and feet. Adjust your outstretched arms and legs so that you maintain your desired approach angle. After your full flare you may want to relax your arms and legs into a modified RW Stable to retain control and reserve stopping power.

Sometimes a side-flare is a handy thing to know. The fast, low angle or at-level approach often results in a hard-to-control flare. When you do a vertical dive and swoop out into a hot low-angle approach, the Relative Wind blows from distinctly ahead and below. Most RW'ers using this approach sit up and then flare. As their speed decreases, the direction of the Relative Wind shifts toward below, necessitating constant changes in body position to maintain the proper Angle of Attack. Also, a full flare used with this approach often results in unwanted lift or "ballooning" which is usually countered by bending the legs up out of the Relative Wind's way. This is inefficient because the legs should be used in braking.

An easy way to counter this unwanted "ballooning" problem, which often seems characteristic of low angle approaches, is to lay over on your side and then flare. Said differently, if you can't maintain a low enough approach angle while in a full flare, don't pull in your legs; rather, rotate your body 90° so that it is presented sideways to the star instead of vertical to it. (Of course you'll want to rotate back to enter.)

Knee braking is used to reduce horizontal velocity when the hands are otherwise occupied, as in docking. A fast hand track can be significantly reduced by bringing the knees down to right angles with the torso.

Fig. 16. Knee Braking.

The RW Turn

A look at your logbook will probably show that wiped-out or bombed stars have a fairly common cause of destruction: a skydiver's inability to dock on wrists. If, instead of wrists, he lands on someone's back or legs, problems immediately arise that result in a small star. It happens because he doesn't know how to make an RW turn.

Not knowing how to use the feet and legs to turn while the hands are occupied, not being able to slide with the star as it rotates show a misunderstanding and inability to do the RW turn.

Turning requires constant awareness of your Angle of Attack and of the Relative Wind. It involves using your whole body "from wingtip to wingtip" to move. That means shoulders, head, thighs, legs and feet are all as involved in flying as are hands. And even more so just prior to docking, as the hands are often occupied in targeting in on wrists.

IN ORDER TO MAKE AN RW TURN YOU MUST USE YOUR ENTIRE BODY AS AN EFFECTIVE DEFLECTOR OF THE WIND. This means you don't use "hands only" student turns. You must feel the Relative Wind, see where you want to go inside your mind and adjust your body to get you there.

Use a bank turn to slide off the Relative Wind in a new direction by dropping the side of your body closest to the direction in which you want to travel and raising the other side. In other words, if you wish to turn to the left, make a banking turn by leaning left.

If you want to go sideways or backwards or diagonally, simply adjust the appropriate parts of your body to an angle which will meet the wind to effect the desired change in direction. If you find you're not moving in the direction you want to, then you aren't deflecting enough air to move. Keep adjusting the deflection surface till you do.

Another RW turn that is similar to the bank turn for use close to the star is the "keel turn." Heavier relative workers may find they lose too much altitude with the bank turn. If so, the keel turn may be their answer.

Execute a keel turn by using your inside leg as a keel on which to turn. Draw up the knee to change the direction of your flight as you stop sliding. This works especially well when the star is turning.

Fig. 17. Keel Turn.

Note that these turns are different from student or style turns which effect a simple change in heading. RW turns effect a change in direction of movement.

RW turns should be practiced. It is important to be able to move in any direction without changing heading. Try flying backwards and sideways. Practice no-hands flying to teach your legs to be as effective as your arms.

Finally, don't try to make turns close to the star using only your arms. Make even the slightest change of direction with an RW turn, banking into the turn properly, coordinating your arms, legs and body. It will make that rough entry much smoother!

Recovery Maneuvers

Until you become so good as to never miss; until you join that exclusive 100% club where you're as good as you already think you are, you have to learn how to get back up to where the star is. You have to learn how to go from below those lucky bastards who didn't go low to a level where you can do effective, fully controlled relative work. For when you are below the star you have all you can handle just to get back up.

Recovery requires all of your surface area. You must use every inch of yourself to recover the altitude you need to enter the formation. You'll have no surface left for deflecting wind to approach the star, so you have to do better than "get up" to its level. You have to be able to get up above it again. When you descend you have gravity to assist; you might say that gravity is sort of a motor which you can use to change your speed. The problem in going up is that you have to fight that gravity.

Even when you become a Skygod you'll need to know recovery maneuvers. I've seen flyers who are so used to getting in every formation on the first try, they are at a loss when something unexpected happens and they find themselves below something.

When you want to "GO UP" you must fully concentrate on doing so and put everything else out of your mind. Body configuration is critical. Every inch of you must come effectively into use.

(It is assumed that you will not try to come up in an area where you are a hazard to the star or other jumpers. Should you foul up an RW jump by getting below the star and loitering there, you should letter the words "Stupid Ass" on your forehead.)

After quickly determining that you're not going to come up into a clumsy area, whip into a flat stable and then into the full reverse arch recovery position.

To do this, think aggressively about going UP! Fast! Put some muscle into it! Here's where you use extreme muscle tension. Reverse your body's arch, not just the arch of your legs and arms; reverse the whole thing. Arch your torso. Concentrate on feeling strong wind resistance against all of your body. Get your shoulders into it. You should be able to see both your hands and feet easily. You should be so intensely reverse-arched that you nearly flutter like a falling leaf. Put your feet sideways, heel to heel.

If you do all this and concentrate on it, you'll bob up like a cork. You'll be surprised at the recovery power you'll have.

Incorrect.

Correct.

Fig. 18. Recovery Position.

There is a recovery-approach technique that is very advanced but can be learned. It gives you the ability to enter the star from a point below the star (not directly below, of course). Since it's tricky and fraught with hazard, it is ordinarily used as a last resort. Keep it well in mind that it is never okay to selfishly take out a star because *you* want to get in.

To do the recovery-approach you rear-up and use your upper body as the recovery area to cup the air. Your forearms, hands and shins deflect the air and generate some forward speed along with the upward speed. You have to feel for this one.

Fig. 19. Recovery—Approach.

RW Across a Vacuum

Sometimes when you're doing "the most perfect final approach the world has ever seen," you'll suddenly find the bottom dropping out. You'll flounder in no air. There is suddenly no buoyant cushion of air for you to work on. You are Falling!

Obviously you've passed over someone below the star, and the vacuum that extends above his back has sucked you down. Or it *will* suck you down unless you react IMMEDIATELY.

Quickly spread all the way out flat and use your hands and feet to creep forward, as in a hand track or recovery-approach. You can probably get out of the vacuum area and perhaps still enter without fully aborting. The trick is to react quickly.

Chapter III
Feeling The Air

"How I yearn to throw myself into endless space and float above the abyss." Goethe .

Get to know the air you fly in—it's the element of freefall. Air is your friend and official RW helper. It gives you a place to skydive and creates fantastic valleys of clouds for your admiration and company as you engage in the exhilarating aerial ballet of relative work.

Touch the air; it can be warm or freezing. Feel it; it can be so soft as to offer no resistance at all or so hard you can hardly stick your arm out in it. Perhaps strangest of all, it's usually blue except on close examination when it's clear (none of this is true in a smog bank).

Hear it. Inside a conch shell it sounds like the sea. In freefall it sounds like the furies of Hell.

Fly on it. Icarus did; you can, too. Next time you swoop, feel the air. It gets thicker and thinner as you perform RW in the sky. In a dive, when you're going fast, it's very thick. During subterminal RW, it seems very thin.

Fig. 20. Icarus.

Air is enlightened water. Buddha said that the One Mind is like the sky. The sky is the somewhat mysterious something you sense when you do freefall. Sometimes you ride the wind. Sometimes you fall like a toad. Feeling the air helps you to ride the wind.

Remember that rocks merely fall while seagulls, stunt planes and skydivers descend. Your flying ability depends on your speed in the air. Your ability to do RW well depends on your awareness of the Relative Wind and your sensing of speed through the Relative Wind instant by instant as you dance toward the formation.

As you feel the wind and test the firmness of the air, you'll change the Angle of Attack of your hand, your leg, or your whole body so that it follows the scenario of your mind. You'll feel it and at the same time you'll notice the effects your movements have on the relative position of your target formation. You'll do all of this with full-on concentration of mind and controlled relaxation of body ...and your every thought will be motion.

Air is like water—you can feel its buoyancy. Your skydiving air is "customized" to you and you can make it as thick or as thin as you wish in order to vary your buoyancy so that you can dive through and maneuver in it at will, just as you can in a pool of water.

This varying of buoyancy is keyed by relaxing your star-crazed mind so that your tactile sense of feel can find the direction and speed of the Relative Wind.

The Mechanics of Feeling the Air

The mechanics of feeling the air's buoyancy are simple if you already know how. Otherwise, it's difficult to get into because it is so subtle. It's rather like smoking pot—people seldom get high on their first experience because they look for some striking, obvious effect on the mind and body, a sort of drunken stupor. If the search for these non-existent effects is intense enough, the real but vastly more subtle effects of the weed are overlooked. To enjoy, you have to relax your mind and let your senses relay their messages.

In freefall it's noisy and confusing. The noise, the loss of an unmoving reference as a guide to your movement, the vertigo...all of these things send booming messages into your brain which demand immediate attention.

Result? All you seem to feel is the sound and the fury. You're very much a stranger in a strange land. Your over-loaded mind and senses can't sort out the confusion, can't rank the incoming messages in any order of importance to flying, and you figuratively blow a fuse, just like any other over-loaded circuit.

I've trained hundreds of students and have seen it happen often. They step out into the blinding sky with its hurricane wind and ever-shifting ground; they watch the plane fall up and BUZZzzzap! they go blank.

As you make more and more jumps you become more of a "native" to the sky. You realize that the sound and the fury are nothing more nor less than the neon lights, congested traffic, swirling crowds and hustle-bustle of any downtown street. Just as you learn to disregard the distracting sights and sounds of a busy city so that you may notice when the traffic light turns from red to green and allows you to safely maneuver to your destination, you have to learn to do the same thing with relative work.

If you filter out the extraneous messages and react only to those signals which help you do RW, you'll be less confused, more relaxed and "better." You will quit spending your limited time and energy on distractions and thus have that much more time and energy for Swoopin'.

The important thing about buoyancy is that it can be sensed. As noted above, this is one of the more hard-to-get-at skills in the whole art of flying—this sensing of "lift," the gauging of the firmness or "substance" of the air. The "feel" you must have to make contact, and the ability to know what your body is actually doing: this we'll call the flying instinct.

The RW'er needs this sense of buoyancy during almost every second of every maneuver. He needs it every time he makes an approach on a formation. How many times have you flared only to find that you were too high and had to try to pick up speed again? How many times have you flared too late and had to circle the star, or go below? Your RW ability depends in large measure upon your ability to sense lift or the loss of it. Most spastic "FUBARS" happen only because the relative worker's sense of buoyancy failed him.

The novice RW'er realizes all of this in a vague way. He knows that he needs this sense and he also knows that he doesn't have it. He feels like a blind man walking in traffic.

A vague feeling of frustration plagues the novice. He feels that something important is being left unsaid; that there is some answer, which if given, would help him over the hump. Unfortunately he has little, if any, orientation; he can't ask the right questions. And even if he did, very few would know how to help him.

We will try to help.

One important cue is speed. The sensing of the air's firmness is almost the same thing as speed. Fast flight means flight at a low angle of attack (steep dives) while slow flight usually means flight at a high angle of attack (handtracking.) Speed equals buoyancy, but speed is difficult to judge.

Air can't be seen, so air speed is difficult to detect except in relation to the freefall formation you're working on. Since it's hard to "see" speed you must enlist your other senses to help your eyes.

A good speed cue in RW is the sound of flight. Subterminal RW in "soft" air is quiet. A full-tilt, no-lift vertical dive is noisy. Even the unskilled ear of the beginning swooper can easily hear and interpret the sounds of flight. Often, however, he doesn't pay attention.

As Langewiesche[4] says, learning to fly largely consists of not developing new senses, but learning to use your old senses for new and different purposes. Particularly, you must get away from the domination of your eyes and make much heavier use of your hearing, your sense of touch, and your inner ear with its feel for acceleration and balance.

Whether your arms and legs experience a hard or soft

[4]*Stick and Rudder*, p. 59.

feel is an excellent clue to airspeed. In a fast dive, the strength required to stick an arm or leg into the airstream is considerable and you need only expose a small portion to the windblast to obtain a considerable reaction. In sub-terminal relative work you'd probably need to use your entire body in exaggerated movement to obtain a like result.

Most RW'ers are aware of this varying feeling of pressure on their arms; many experienced RW'ers feel it on their legs, too. The best RW'ers feel changes in pressure, buoyancy and speed with their feet, ankles, shins, thighs, pelvis, upper and lower torso, shoulders, arms, hands and head. The desirability of getting full available feel has led to the use of tennis shoes, thin or no gloves, and soft helmets among some relative workers—all for better feel of the air.

Testing the Cushion

Accurate sensing of one's buoyancy is especially important during final approach and docking in the star, particularly if the approach is on a squirrelly or poorly flown star. The RW flyer then seeks just exactly the right amount of buoyancy and horizontal movement. A slight reserve of lift is necessary so that when he arrives at the star he will be able to flare, check his descent, and have just enough reserve buoyancy to cope with a moving star.

How to have exactly the right amount of buoyancy to take care of such a situation? It involves knowing whether you have a cushion of reserve lift, whether the final flare before docking will result in enough lift to check your approach, or whether you will overamp and go below. The best way to find out is to test your flare just a tad early and watch how you and the star behave. You must judge the effect not only by eye, but by kinesthesia with every muscle and tendon. Note the small changes in your weight, the feelings of lightness or heaviness of pressure, and your angle of closure with the star... these are all clues to your buoyancy.

Your perception of balance and relative speed is very

sensitive—provided you pay attention to them. A large part of the art of flying consists of paying attention to the seemingly odd things that really do matter.

Skydivers "feel" for lift almost continuously during their final approach—especially in the last stages where their coast or glide blends into the actual docking.

Try out each of these clues separately. Remember, there is a great difference between merely perceiving something with your senses and **noticing** it. In the situation given earlier, a jungle-dwelling primitive transplanted to an American city street would see traffic lights just as you do—maybe even better. But he would probably overlook them and watch instead the flashing neon signs, pretty store windows and other more impressive things that are much less important than the traffic light.

We see the traffic signs even while thinking of something else because we watch for them and we understand their meaning instantly. We know that, though they are not very attention-catching, they are important.

"The clues by which we fly, the things our senses must pick up in order to enable us to fly, are all perfectly plain, and can be easily and plainly perceived by eyes, ears and so forth, of less than average keenness. Our difficulty in learning to (do RW) is not sense perception, but interpretation of what our senses perceive. We tend to pay attention to the wrong things; we miss the things that matter because we aren't looking for them, because we do not know what they mean."[5]

The process of learning RW would be quicker and surer if novice RW'ers knew more clearly what to watch for. Experienced RW'ers should take time to point out more precisely just what it is the student is supposed to learn. Sometimes it's a clearer idea of the mechanics of flight that is needed. Sometimes it's a clearer idea of what his own body is actually doing. We must teach our students to use their fine senses when learning RW.

Show a student RW'er what the clues are and why they are important, and he won't be such a toad. Once his attention has dwelled on them a few times they become

[5]*Stick and Rudder*, p. 72.

much more noticeable; once the correct response to them has been **practiced** formally a few times, it becomes almost automatic. And that is all the so-called "flying instinct" consists of: small clues, understood correctly, and reacted to automatically.

Stability

Stability is such a basic part of freefall RW it hardly seems worth mentioning, but we'd better.

Everybody who does relative work can fall stable, of course. Are you sure? Stability is more than just going into the student arch and not spinning. Stability in RW connotes the ability to maintain control throughout the entire freefall sequence.

Can you always maintain stability without bobbing in a hard dive? Do all your transfers from dives to approaches come off smoothly with never a washout? If you occasionally do have a momentary stability problem, you will soon solve it yourself. But you will solve it a lot sooner if you think out "stability" before jumping. Importantly, you will be more relaxed as you learn the other so-called "critical" RW maneuvers.

One of the positions that lends itself to smooth RW maneuver transitions is the relaxed RW Stable which was explained under maneuvers in Chapter II. The reason this position is so stable is simple... you aren't doing anything to mess it up. You perfect it by doing less.

The whole objective of the RW Stable is to give you a base maneuver with a vertical speed you can vary at will to make a transition into another RW maneuver without undue gymnastics. The method is simply to totally relax your body so that your arms and legs blow behind you in the wind. You relax your hands and feet so they are limp and don't induce any turns. You relax your back and shoulders; you let your head blow back. You are fully "resting" on the wind.

The RW Stable position is worth learning. Don't forget to notice the color of the sky, or the rush of a puffy cloud while you're learning it. Or better yet, go up with a friend and learn it together.

It's nice to give yourself fully to the wind—and then work it gently as it tells you its endless story.

Using the Relative Wind on Exit.   Pat Works.

Chapter IV
What It Means to Fly

 When you go up into the air you lose your connection with the solid ground and its comfortable, constant visual indicators of speed and movement—things like the lines on the highway, passing fenceposts and trees, etc. These provide ready reference points that are generally unchanging. Leave these familiar earth-bound surroundings where the only directions you need worry about are right and left, forward and backward, and things are apt to get confusing.

In RW you can fly in an up-and-down sense as well as in a right-and-left sense. There are no familiar visual landmarks to tell you much about your movement. What makes it most confusing is that you are trying to connect with another object also falling in this unmarked, undifferentiated void.

I can't think of another sport like it. In motor racing, the corners stay put as you approach them. In tennis, the ground and the net stay in the same place to give you visual clues to your position and movement. Relative work lacks these clues.

In RW the relationship of the horizon and the formation does give you a rough clue of where you are. If the horizon is well above the star, then you are well above the star. If the horizon is below it, then so are you.

A better indicator is the shape of the star or formation. If you are above it you can see clearly everyone's backs; if you are at a 45° angle to it you will see some backs and some faces. If you are level, you'll see sides of legs within a narrow angle of view, and if you are below the star you'll see stomachs.

Viewed from directly above.

Viewed from at level.

Viewed from below (hopefully seldom!).

Viewed from a 45° angle.

Fig. 21.

Another confusing element when you're approaching a star is the relationship between your height above the formation, your speed and the required maneuver necessary to approach and dock to enter. (This is covered more fully in the chapter on approaches.)

Here is where the visual clues described earlier are tied into your feel of the Relative Wind. It sounds complex, and is. But so is catching a ball, driving a car or any other physical activity requiring motor coordination. What is hard about RW is not this complexity, because your mind can easily deal with far more complex situations, but your unfamiliarity with the situation. You don't know which clues to react to, so you try to "think it out" while you are trying to *do* it. Trial and error plus understanding (and lots of jumps) eventually show the best way and you reach your goal. It's like learning to catch a ball.

When you fly, concentrate on perfection in flying rather than on reaching a goal such as "getting in fast," and you will do better. Relax your mind so that it can receive the sensations of flying which will key the correct response.

Pay particular attention to the size and shape of the RW formation. It will provide your mind with the required data.

If you have trouble docking—if you can get very close but just don't have enough steam to get onto wrists, or conversely, if you're hitting too hard—then you are not controlling your speed. Either you lack enough momentum to dock properly, or you have too much momentum and are endangering the formation. If you can't hit wrists but wind up on legs or backs, see the discussion of RW turns in the chapter on maneuvers.

There are two ways to gain speed. First, you can start out high and convert your altitude into speed: the steeper and farther you go down, the more speed you pick up. At the level of the formation you convert this downward speed into enough horizontal speed to dock. (This is momentum RW.) Or, you can start at-level with the star and hand-track toward it. Here your speed is generated by redirecting the wind.

Both of these methods require feeling the Relative Wind and reacting to its signals while at the same time concentrating on the size and shape of the RW formation. Changes in its size and shape are indicators of your relative position and speed. You must also watch for the formation's relative movement. Since it probably won't stay put you must continually compensate by going toward the spot where it is going to be when you get there.

All of this is what makes the final approach and docking-entry seem so difficult. I maintain that attention to and perfection of the basic RW maneuvers will make approaches and docking almost easy.

Approaches simply show up flaws in your basic RW technique—flaws that otherwise go undetected. If your mastery of flight is firm enough you'll have little trouble with the "advanced" RW techniques. If you really know how to fly an RW turn and how to fly at various angles of attack, you are probably good at RW.

"Hard" vs. "Soft" RW

In momentum RW, you never stop or overly slow down your approach until entry. This redirection of track/descent-generated velocity is controlled largely by your mental attitude and "set." Your actions are choreographed by your imagination and you fly with the "power center" in the middle of your stomach. All of which is a constant for you, but varies between jumpers as individuals. (More on this "power center" later.)

There are various ways of approaching the subject of momentum relative work. Likewise, there are two different schools of karate: "hard" or "soft." In "hard" karate, a powerful direction of energy is used to achieve the desired result. In "soft" karate, the desired result is achieved by *re*directing the energy of the onslaught. Relative work uses these "hard" and "soft" definitions in much the same way.

An example of "hard" RW would be the hard flare against the propwash on exit, a strong and furious blind-dive and arch-out swoop at the rushing star, with a balls-out, gut-wrenching flare that puts you on wrists with a snatch-grip to enter immediately.

In "soft" RW you exit, feel the propwash, and flare against its push to a head-high, directly-at-the-star delta. Your chest is held high for lift. Your swoop seems gentle but you keep on cooking in, and your sit-up is only for the entry.

The difference? In hard RW you go faster from exit to flare point. In soft RW you go slower from exit point to flare point, but your time from exit to entry is averagely equal to the "hard" approach. Some prefer this soft RW because if approached correctly, it eliminates personal mistakes even when the star is floating or moving. Hard RW, on the other hand, feels faster.

Again, execution of any kind of relative work requires mastery of all the basic modes of flight as a minimum. This mastery is doubly important. First, it gives you the physical ability and coordination required to perform the maneuvers, and secondly, it gives you the mental confidence in this ability to single-pointedly enter into flight for the joy of flying. When you look at it like that, how can the result be other than satisfying?

Although complete mastery of RW techniques requires effort, it will happen. For in addition to the released energy of your own efforts, you are further assisted by the energy flow from everyone else in the formation who, because you are on the load with them, want you to do well.

Here, then, is the likely cause of much bad flying by experienced jumpers: it originates within their own mind. Everyone in any true sport faces this challenge. The best solution to it is to have the relaxed but attentive attitude of a sharp-eyed eagle diving for slow-moving prey in a vast expanse of ether. SWOOOOP!!! Dinner is served!

Take advantage of our musically-oriented generation. Listen to the music you like. Let your mind's eye hear the symphony, or the rock music, and let your imagination fly as the pertinent signals come in. In the same way, let your mind's eye receive the pertinent signals of relative work. Dig the colors of the formation, the movement and the flash of blue sky.

Multi-person RW sometimes leaks an over-abundance of Ego and fear of poor self-performance. What's needed is reassertion of your true purpose for doing relative work...JOY!

Worrying about what will happen "if," and lamenting what did happen "then," are indulgences. "If" is the Future. "Then" is the Past. Only the act of RW is now. Do RW in the Present.

Fly to the Tune of Your Senses

To enter a star smoothly you must be relaxed with your body, aggressive with your mind, controlled by your will. Skydiving requires precise control of the body. Making it do what you will it to do *when* you will it to happen; knowing where your feet, arms, head and other parts of the body are at all times.

The mind must be controlled at the same time. The mind is a sophisticated sense reader telling you what your body feels and sees. Uncontrolled, it dwells on tension or fear of making a mistake or other destructive thoughts. Destructive thoughts they are, because they take away some of the attention and mental energy of the mind.

If you are to properly coordinate mind and body into precision relative work you must have all your mental energy directed toward one goal: the exhilarating perfection of an art.

In relative work you use your senses—touch, "feeling" the air, sight, sound—all feed data to your mind. Your mind sorts and correctly analyzes this data and the resulting action is more perfect flight.

The mind should be single-pointed so that all the subtle and uncommon sense signals of RW may be received and read. Do not clutter up your flying with fear, tension, ego or pride. Use your will to direct your mind toward performing each movement well. All of the movements, properly performed, will result in superior

RW. Speed will come after ability and skill. Being close does not count; only being THERE fulfills the task.

RW'ers naturally tend to stay in good physical shape; few good RW'ers are flabby and out of condition. Dancing, tennis, skiing and other recreations will sharpen your reactions and senses; disciplines such as yoga and karate improve the will as well. Can you balance on one foot? Can you dance smoothly without looking spastic? Why not?

If the advancement of RW skills through the use of the will to control the mind and body sounds rather mysterious, then let's look at it another way: mental attitude. A good mental attitude helps your flying. A good mental attitude is one that dotes on the beauty of the air—its colors and clouds. A good mental attitude is luxuriating in the dancing, sinewy movements of RW which, in perfection, are pleasure and beauty in themselves. A good mental attitude is a joyful swoop and rush on the star. This attitude toward doing what you love to do helps you to be good at that endeavor because it leaves the mind in a receptive state for reading the many subtle but important messages that instrument freefall relative work.

Myself, I try to dig the beauty of the sky and clouds as we line up to exit. On exit I imagine myself dancing to the music of the wind and savor each movement for its pleasure and expression. It works.

Another friend becomes in his mind's eye an eagle. Another becomes a ballet dancer, another a seagull, others just go to it. The positive attitude is what is important. **You can do RW if you only let yourself do it.**

Red is a friend of mine who digs RW. Once I overheard him talking to some RW novices:

"Some day it's gonna happen to you. I'm telling it like it is...someday you're going to enter the star and you'll feel the electricity that runs through it. It'll blow your mind! Everybody'll be diggin' it just like you do and you'll be able to feel it. I know; it happens all the time."

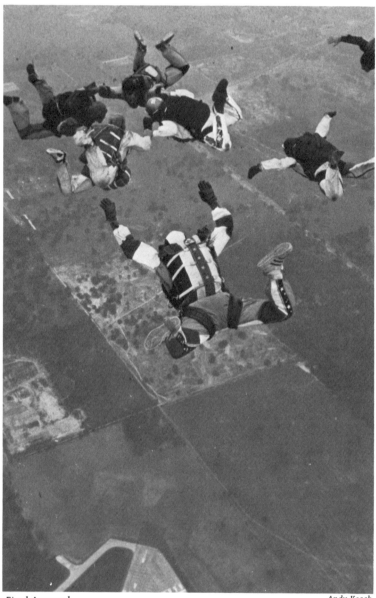

Final Approach.   Andy Keech.

Chapter V
Approaches

The Descent Approaches

There are three basic approach angles from the aircraft to the star used in momentum RW. There are really two categories of approaches: 1) the descent approach, and 2) the docking or final approach.

The first is used from exit until you set up on final to dock; the second is the final attack technique you use to smoothly enter the star. Note that what the jumper thinks is happening on any of the descent approaches is often contrary to what is actually happening. In any exit you retain the momentum of the aircraft. This built-in speed of 80-100 knots carries you horizontally along with the aircraft until it is dissipated.

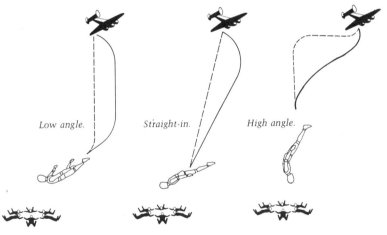

Low angle.   *Straight-in.*   *High angle.*

Fig. 22. Descent Approaches.
    What he thinks he is doing. – – – –
    What he is actually doing. ———

Thus, after exit, while your vertical descent remains constant your horizontal speed toward the star will vary with the speed of the airplane and your recognition of this momentum effect. Importantly, for the first 1-6 seconds after exit the Relative Wind blows distinctly from the direction in which the aircraft is moving, miscalled the "prop wash" effect. Remember this.

In the low-angle descent approach you exit and go into a vertical or no-lift dive for 7-9 seconds; then you arch into a delta and swoop in on the star until you reach your flare point. At the flare point you throw out all your laundry to reduce your closing speed and then come in on final to dock and enter. You'll probably want to use the side-flare for the best braking effect.

The flare point and amount of flare is important but the amount of time in the vertical dive is more so. If you dive too long you'll find yourself way below the star (and even if you get in, your approach from below will likely take out someone behind you who falls into your vacuum.) Coming out of the dive too soon wastes time, too. If you use a low-angle descent approach, take these variables into consideration.

Also, in a hot level-with-the-star approach in the sitting-up "mush" position, it's possible to stall out and fall off the air if your horizontal speed gets low and you fail to correct for it by adapting to the downward shifting change in the Relative Wind. Stalls are avoided by your constant awareness of changes in the Relative Wind.

A "mush" is a braking position in which you descend on the star, your body presented at an angle to it. Often after flaring you'll have both vertical and horizontal velocity remaining from your descent dive. You fly in the mush position to compensate for the resulting Relative Wind angles.

The 45° or straight-in approach means what it says. Your purpose is to go from the airplane door to the star in as straight a line as possible. You exit and immediately head for the star, keeping your eye on it and boogie as fast as you can.

Fig. 23. "Mush" position.

Your flare will be a little easier to handle than with the low-angle approach, probably due in part to a lower approach speed. But mainly a flare from a 45° descent approach is easier because there is little shift in the direction of the Relative Wind as your velocity decreases. A mush is also commonly used with this approach.

The high-angle approach is the reverse of the low-angle approach. You exit and first concentrate on killing all aircraft-generated momentum before heading for the area way above the top of the star in a max-track. Your purpose is to cover maximum horizontal distance first.

As you approach the area way above the top of the star, bend at the waist and do a vertical dive. Your approach speed on the star will be fast and scary. When you flare, however, you can do a full flare with few complications.

In the high-angle approach, the Relative Wind's direction stays more or less constantly below you (instead of shifting from ahead and below to below, as in the low-angle approach.) However, high-angle approaches must level out close to the star or mishaps are likely. You must also remember that you retain forward motion from the initial max-track. Your dive should be a tad short of the star, or this leftover speed will put you too close.

In each of the above approaches there is a point *outside* the star, somewhere from knees to 30 feet out, where your descent approach ends and you start your final approach to dock and enter. Where this point is depends on your experience, skill, and where your head is.

With the low-angle approach you are more or less committed to a point outside a particular quadrant of the star. With the 45° you can opt for any slot on your half of the star and still get a "straight-in" final. Using the high-angle approach you can pick a spot anywhere around the star during your dive or flare without causing traffic problems. However, there's a chance that someone may move in under you on a lower approach and cause problems for you.

★   ★   ★   ★   ★   ★   ★   ★

Mirror, Mirror, watch my fall.
Tell me please,
The best approach of them all?

Which is the best descent approach for you? Good question. All are used by some very fast people. There doesn't seem to be any standard correlation between body size/weight and the descent approach technique to be used, though some generalizations can be made.

For going early out of a small-door airplane (slots 3 thru 6) the 45° is very good. The 45° approach is also used by some very consistently fast people. The low-angle approach is the oldest and "most natural" but it is hard to flare with. The high-angle approach is fast but scary; you may need to be a low-mass floater type to use it well.

Large-door aircraft in conjunction with a *fast* exit

seem to require the 45° or the high-angle descent approach. Speed isn't desired here because the exit is so fast. The problem is NOT getting there fast. You are already there!—in a big gob with ten other people. The problem then becomes traffic jams and fast entries. Horizontal distance is shorter, the base is much closer and you usually don't have time to build up the speed required for a fast low-angle approach.

Out of small-door aircraft, your exit is spread out and you can opt for any of the approaches. I think the classic low-angle approach is the easiest to start with but it demands a considerable amount of finesse as you approach your limit.

The 45° is initially a bit harder to master but seems to be very consistent. The newest approach, the high-angle, really hasn't been tested yet. It offers several theoretical advantages in the area of control but is difficult for novices to work with.

You can practice any of these approaches out of nearly any aircraft you can do RW out of. If you're jumping a C-182 and want to simulate going tenth out of a small door Twin Beech, just wait 4 seconds after everyone else leaves. Then go and learn your thing.

The Final Approach

After a few fast approaches on a star, the novice RW'er soon realizes how difficult flying into a star can be. Your body has a perverse way of not going where you are trying to make it go.

Actually all of the RW maneuvers are hard to do precisely, but most of them are performed well away from any reference point so that the sorry lack of control we have does not show up as clearly. The final approach, however, takes you out of those empty spaces of air and puts you close to other descending skydivers near the small target of wrists. When you first start trying to hit your target, it's easy to overshoot or undershoot by a wide margin.

The difficulties of the final approach are twofold. One

is the problem of depth perception—the inexperienced eye cannot gauge exactly where the body is going. The other difficulty is a problem of control—in an approach maneuver what you must get your body to do in order to get in often seems directly contrary to "common sense."

For example, as you approach wrists in momentum RW and see that you are going to miss, you will take the corrective action that seems "natural." If you're going to overshoot you will "naturally" want to dive downward toward wrists. But this natural reaction will only make you overshoot still more because it mainly serves to speed up your rate of horizontal movement and thus carry you over the top of the star, much to your confusion.

What you should do in this situation seems counter to your common sense, but it works. A flare and backslide will cause your body to fall more vertically, thus reducing your horizontal speed.

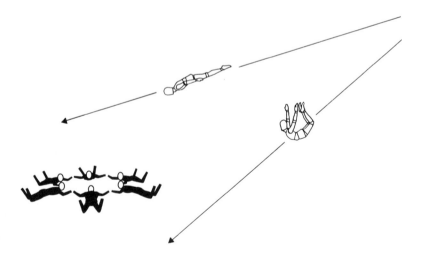

Fig. 24. Momentum RW Final Approach. If you want to come down more steeply, use an RW Stable or a backslide. If you want to come down less steeply, max-track.

You must understand how your approach can be controlled. It's simple. In momentum RW, when you are close to the star and want to go down more steeply, either flare your arms and tuck your legs to backslide, or relax into the RW Stable. If you want to go down less steeply because you are going to undershoot, put your arms back and assume the max-track position.

All of this runs contrary to one's experience with automobiles, sleds, boats and other ground vehicles. And since it is contrary to past experience, it's hard to do the right thing when the time comes. But if you think about it, it does make sense. If you understand the reasons why, it won't be so hard to do.

When practicing final approaches, use the same angle and rate of speed each time. There are good reasons for being constant. Visual judgment during the approach is difficult for the novice to master, and its parameters differ with each type of momentum RW approach. It introduces too many perception variables into a situation that is confused enough.

Experienced RW'ers often vary their approach considerably, depending on exit order or the timing of the exit, but the novice will do well to find an approach "groove" and stick to it while learning.

It is especially important to keep your body in a constant half-flared coasting configuration on final approach. Set up as far out as you can and then coast "down the pipe" to the star, making smooth corrections all the way. Keep your eyes on the target wrists. Be aware of what your legs are doing. Fly straight into the star because last second turns are very hard to gauge.

Final Approach Angle

The experienced relative worker sees the ground below him as a huge bowl, the brim being the horizon. When a star or other RW formation is in the distance it is difficult to tell how far away it is except by its size. What serves the RW'er best is to think: "This star is 45° below me." If this angle decreases drastically you are going to be low on your final approach unless you are already close. If this angle increases, you are going to be too high. This is another judgment to be considered when setting up your final approach.

As you come in on final approach, things start to happen fairly fast. Even if you are right in the groove for a good, solid docking, you will probably encounter some star movement requiring constant adjustments. Make them fast. It is much easier to make corrections 10-20 ft. away from the star rather than close in.

How can you judge if you're going to make it? One clue is an old accuracy trick. Check the apparent motion of your target—wrists. Two things will be happening at once. First, the star is growing rapidly in apparent size because you are approaching it. At the same time, all of the star will show some motion as it grows.

Keep your eyes on wrists and remember this: if your target wrists move downward, however slightly, you are going to overshoot; if the wrists move upward you are about to undershoot. You will easily contact the objects that remain stationary in your field of vision. It's just like shooting accuracy—with the disc moving in three dimensions!

Borrow another accuracy technique to make sure you'll make it. Set up your approach so that you know you can reach the far side of the star in your trajectory. You can always use more brakes but you can't get more drive as easily if you need it.

Another good key is the way things look when everything is going well. Next time you are in a star, check out how the people across the star from you appear. Set this in your mind. They will look the same way, i.e. have the same perspective, every time. When you're about to dock and enter, check what you see; if it doesn't look right, it probably is not right.

Chapter VI
Docking & Flying the Star

The whole symphony of freefall relative work is shaped toward the crescendo of entry into the formation, or docking. This instant of contact with your brother and sister flyers must be precisely executed. In other maneuvers a relative worker can continually correct his mistakes as they become apparent to him. The final approach, for example, is usually a series of small corrections. At the moment of contact with the star, however, any error becomes alarmingly apparent to everyone involved. To avoid mistakes, embarrassment and small stars, you should know how to dock and enter.

The first bit of confusion arises outside the star—what is the correct speed for closing? If you go in too slowly you will bounce off the air (burble) around the star and won't be able to get in. If you go a little too fast you will set the star into a wobbly mess or even tear it to pieces.

If you bobble or shake up the star your sloppiness gives your ego a beating. If you tear up a star, you suffer doubly. For one thing, you know you've messed up and you feel badly about it. You've also messed up the jump for the other jumpers and they usually feel compelled to give you a verbal lashing. As a result you're even more tense the next time, and since tenseness makes for bad RW it's then easy to do worse. The cycle repeats itself on the next jump and it will seem as if the sun has stopped shining for you.

On the other hand, a timid docking is no better. You wash around in the slot and end up reaching, floating and bouncing off people.

For the beginner it is no simple task to fly and dock when going very slowly. It requires visual judgment that comes only with practice. The star's movements seem magnified. Also, a slow approach and entry usually means you're using a lot of body surface to generate speed. On touching the star, this large surface exposure makes you float in the slot. You can't seem to keep your ass down and you thrash around most unprofessionally. You're tense and it shows as you flap like a dishtowel drying on a clothesline.

Relax. Do relative work with the star. Let your hips, legs and feet go limp; this will get your ass down. Loosen your pectoral muscles and allow your chest to settle down between your shoulders and arms. Then shake and break to enter.

Another cause of poor docking is the novice's delayed reaction to the changing situation. He fumbles at flying when he should be relaxing to integrate himself with the movements of the star. In RW movies, a bad docking looks comic. In *your* RW, it causes small stars and unfriendly talk.

Try approaching the star in a normal glide and level out just outside the star so that you are shooting along dead level with a bit of excess speed. As you enter the slot your level approach will not allow the star to shift under you since you'd bump off their sides first. Keep your hands and arms bent in front of you, fingers ready to grasp. Use your shoulders and legs and head and ass to help you fly your entire body.

Remember that you must do bank turns or slide to effect a change in direction if you find the star, or yourself, orbiting.

Let your speed carry you onto wrists. Do not reach. If you are going to hit solidly, cushion your entry by docking with your forearms, elbows and hands to distribute the shock and avoid bending the star inward.

Analysis of RW photos and movies shows that most good dockings are made with knees down. The final approach may be from any angle, but on contact with the star, docking, the knees are down.

The reason for this is simple. When you break wrists, you naturally spread out your arms. This is a flared position and you'll "float." If your body is level or a little ass-high, this slight float will wash you up in the slot. If you tense up at this critical moment, you can flip over the star. If you are slow in relaxing into the slot, you will be sloppy. Get your knees down to avoid all that.

Elements of Docking

1. Make a level final approach (the last five to ten feet.)
2. Do not reach.
3. Take up docking shock with your forearms.
4. Preliminarily grab wrists.
5. Settle into the slot, get your ass down, fly with the star.
6. Finalize your grip.
7. Shake and break to enter the star.
8. Smile. (Ear to ear.)

Do each step in order. Don't try to skip a step. Later your entry will smooth out and seem to be a single, nearly instantaneous motion. But for the time being, learn the basics and apply them.

Using Depth Perception

Some of the judgment you will use in docking maneuvers is based on depth perception. Depth perception results from our having two eyes set apart in our head. This stereo vision provides a perception of distance.

Pure depth perception works only at about 100 feet or closer. But you also use indirect depth perception, such as size of objects, shape, perspective, etc. to determine distances. These indirect means of determining distance can be learned.

To understand how you visually judge your altitude, try jumping in the east and then move to the desert. It's easy to misjudge your altitude if you set up a landing over shrubs that you thought were really trees. It is well documented that water presents even greater problems.

Thus you have both direct and indirect clues with which to judge depth and, indirectly, speed (rate of depth change). Since these indicators require experience to recognize, they must be practiced, even by people who have perfect vision.

The fact that even one-eyed RW'ers can dock and enter demonstrates that judgment of closeness in docking can be broken down into learnable detail. It becomes easy if you know what to look for.

How to Judge a Docking

As you approach the star, keep your vision relaxed and your peripheral vision tuned in. Take in the whole star and the people entering it. Keep moving. Notice their relative size and perspective—their angle to you. Each relative worker in your visual picture can appear in a particular perspective only from a certain height. A single glance tells you how high you are above the formation.

Try it—look at RW photos—you can judge the photographer's height and angle fairly accurately by looking at the perspective of the people in the picture.

Experienced relative workers may say "I don't use that stuff..." though they probably do but without conscious effort. But then this book is for novice RW'ers who want to become "experienced" faster than those of us who learned by experimentation. Again, it is a matter of knowing what to look for; once you recognize it, it becomes nearly reflexive and you will cease having to consciously watch for it.

As you make your final approach, watch perspective indicators of whether you are rising or sinking on the star. The slightest rise will warn you that your relative fall is too slow. You may be too "big," or tense and stiff. In that case, relax into the RW Stable position and sink back to the proper level.

The slightest sink will warn you that your relative fall is too fast—too "heavy," or too tight. Spread out a bit. If your speed slackens, induce a glide into your spreadout position.

Your indicator of rise and sink—a sensitive indicator—is the perspective of the star before you. How, then, do you gauge docking, closing speed and such? You usually tend to try to watch everything at the same time: height, speed, body attitude and star movement. This is interesting but useless.

The thing to watch while docking is the intended docking spot—wrists—and secondly, the people around your target and the perspective in which they appear.

Momentum

You need momentum while docking—excess speed which you dissipate till you're going only a bit too fast, say 10 per cent, just before you reach wrists. Use the cushioned entry described on page 58.

Perhaps the star will move and you'll need this extra measure of speed to follow your slot and dock. Speed/ momentum on docking helps in two ways. It gives you quick, positive control in all respects, and it docks you firmly, allowing your ass and center of gravity to sink below the level of your arms before you enter.

Docking Maneuvers

Your contribution toward building the RW formation starts when you first touch it. Any flying that you do outside and around the star which unfairly impedes others is not acceptable.

All too often novices equate touching the formation with nearly being "in." Poppycock! Making contact with the star means nothing unless you can fly in close formation with it and not disturb its flying.

The structural integrity of the formation must always out-rank your ego-centered desire to be "in." That is why, as mentioned already, the very first thing you must do when you get close to wrists is to settle in with the group before you make contact. Get your ass down, relax your

legs, don't kick, un-bow and relax your shoulders, verify
your grip. Then you will feel that you are part of the star.
Only then should you shake and break to enter.

After 50 or so stars this whole process will take only
part of a second. But until you get that experience, be sure
to settle, dock and relax before you break. Otherwise you
may take the star out or wash it about so badly that it
either self-destructs or becomes so unstable no one else
can safely enter. Contrarily, if you make contact and can't
get settled into the slot, you can usually let go and flare
back out for a better re-docking.

If you tend to sink in your slot after docking, correct
your position of relative fall to maintain altitude and stay
level with your side of the formation. If a full flare (legs
outstretched, spread apart) with reverse arch won't do the
trick, then you aren't doing it properly (ask an experienced
relative worker), or you need a bigger jumpsuit.

The most common docking problem novice RW'ers
encounter is floating in the slot. All too frequently the
inexperienced RW'er will enter the slot a bit too slow and
the "burble" will stop him just short of wrists. Frantically
he reaches and makes "contact." But the act of reaching
increases his effective size which decreases his rate of fall
so that he begins to float. More frantically he tightens his
grip and holds on to ride it out, usually straightening his
legs in the effort. This causes increased floating which
pulls his side of the formation up and pushes it toward the
center.

As his ass and legs rise higher he holds on tighter,
bowing his shoulders to get a "better" grip. This causes
still more floating and he flips through the center or falls
on someone's back. Or someone else may try to enter and
the wobbly star collapses. Or tension on the star gets so
bad that someone else, usually on the other side of the star,
drops a grip. In any event a mess always results and
everyone falls into the tunnel of a funnel.

Let's replay that mess and assume our nervous novice
can follow advice. First, when he finds his approach speed
to be too slow to get him onto wrists, he should flare into

Going too slowly to
penetrate the "burble",
'A' reaches to make contact.

Reaching causes him to float up.
Reaching down in panic now,
he floats even more.

He tightens his grip and unconsciously straightens his
legs at the same time. His shoulders are bowed, like this:

The result is a small star.

Fig. 25. Docking: The Wrong Way.

recovery and fly backwards up and out of the slot, then dipping forward to gain momentum for a proper redocking.

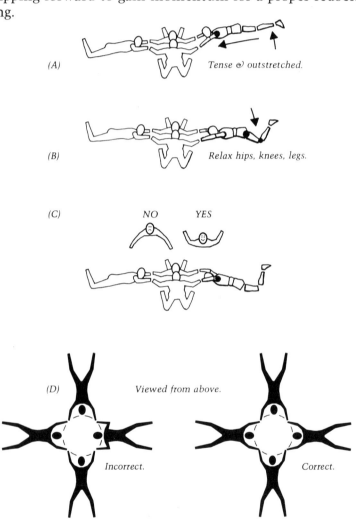

(A)   *Tense & outstretched.*

(B)   *Relax hips, knees, legs.*

(C)   NO   YES

(D)   *Viewed from above.*

Incorrect.   *Correct.*

Fig. 26. Docking: The Right Way.

If he is stiff with outstretched legs, bowed arms, tense body and confused mind, (Fig. 26-A) he should consciously calm his mind as he wills his legs, knees and hips to relax, letting the wind blow them up out of the way (Fig. 26-B). He should then relax his shoulders, letting his head and chest sink lower than his arms (Fig. 26-C). If he finds he is still floating he should push his head and body away from the center toward the outside of the ring of hands. This will pivot his body downward (Fig. 26-D).

He'll be stable enough to enter after any one of these actions although all these maneuvers may need to be called into play. If his side of the star tends to push in toward the center, making the circle an oval, he should throw his head back, too.

In a good entry the axis of the body intersects the center of the star, perpendicular to a tangent line drawn across wrists. In other words, be sure you are headed straight into the slot. All too often, when entering a turning star, a novice will simply turn his head and change only his heading to follow the slot around, while his body continues in the original direction. These types of entries are not often successful. Remember, RW turns must accomplish a change in direction of movement, not just a change of heading alone. This is where a bank turn is necessary.

Grips

When the time comes to take a grip, try to be precise in your hand placement. Aim for wrists. If your hands are suited to it and the wrist you grasp is not too large, wrist grips are fine. A jumpsuit grip is preferred for small hands. Belled jumpsuits offer handy gripping surfaces. When you make a jumpsuit grip, reach over the wrist area to grab the loose fabric on the inside surface. For security and added strength, twist the material in your hands to "lock in."

Getting a good, firm grip is important, but novices frequently concentrate so much on the grip they stiffen and forget to fly. Don't forget to fly your body and use your mind while your hands are occupied with getting a good grip.

If you lose grips often you should be doing hand-strengthening exercises. Get a couple of sponge rubber balls. Have one at home and keep one in your car. Squeeze 'em to strengthen fingers and hands.

Flying the Star

After you've successfully entered, you immediately start a new phase of relative work flying—contact RW, or flying the star. Start out with a good grip.

When you're settled be sure your elbows are at a 90° angle and that your side of the star is level with the opposite side. Your job is to keep your arms at this angle and the star round and level to make it easy for others to enter.

Fig. 27. Maintain 90° arm angle to fly the star.

Holding your arms at 90° reduces the possibility of someone losing a grip. Try this on the ground. Have a friend hold his arm at 90° while you simulate an entry. Now put tension on the grip—it's easy to hold on. If he straightens his arm, however, it becomes very hard to hold on. Be sure your arms are at 90° as you fly the star.

The main trick to flying the star is to relax. Everything you do in the star is also being done by the people beside you, and then must be countered by those across the star, then re-countered by you. If everyone relaxes, very slow, smooth, relaxed corrections will keep the star perfect. Learn to fly *with* the star—it's a big part of RW. If the star isn't being flown well, those outside it will have difficult entries, making it an even worse flying star.

On stars larger than a three-man, never take a base down to "help out" someone who has gone below. This nearly always hurts the final star much more than it helps because you will be making it harder for those who have already set up their final approach by changing the position of the star.

While inside the star your job is to fly the star to make it as easy as possible for **everyone** else on the load to get in. The guy who missed will have to take care of himself; he'll get there or learn something about approaches and reverse arch for his next jump. In the meantime the star will have a chance to build to its maximum size with maximum enjoyment for all (except you-know-who).

If everyone flying a star bends his knees and sits up to increase tension on the star, the star will be stronger and better able to withstand hard-hitting entries. However, this should be done only for stars of ten people or less because it puts increased tension on grips. Larger stars should be flown in "neutral."

Don't try to fly the whole star by yourself. Relative work is the sharing of an experience which requires synchronized movement among a lot of people. **Relax, don't overfly, pay attention, feel the vibes, dig it.**

Exit from a C-130.   *Carl Boenish.*

Chapter VII
Exits from Large Aircraft

Exit ... leave the plane ... bombout ... none of these words convey the energy and coordinated scrambling of the sprinting pell-mell rush through the door of a twin-engine aircraft on a large-star jump.

You know what I mean if you've ever felt the power and emotion of a competition exit. It's an awesome attempt to have the shortest distance possible between the front man and the last man in the lineup with the most miniscule amount of time elapsing between the first and the last man leaving the door.

The exit is beyond question the most important part of a speed star. The exit has more effect on your recorded star time in competition than any other element of the jump. Most championship 10-man teams agree that fully 70-80 per cent of your recorded time on a jump is directly related to your exit time.

In speed stars forget notions about good airwork being key. Remember that all good speed-star teams do their airwork well. The only place there's room to reduce speed-star times when everyone is flying at peak is to speed up the exit. I repeat, the exit is the most important part of a jump for time.

The minutest gap somewhere in the exit doubles itself with each person behind it. Thus even a fraction of a second reduction in exit time will give you stars that are several seconds faster.

The overwhelming importance of exits means you must concentrate four times as hard on them. Several practice exits should be made before **every** load until the exit and lineup "feel" right to everyone. When it is too windy to jump, many teams practice exits with their gear

on. If you have a team member who won't or can't get
enthusiastic about fast exits and the practice of them,
either help him to improve or remove him from the team.
It *is* that important if the team is serious about competition. If your group can't manage perfect teamwork on the
exit, you won't be able to make really fast speed stars.

Theory of a Fast Exit

The ideal exit has three important characteristics:

1) The *shortest amount of distance possible* between
   the first man and the last man in the lineup.
2) On exit, this distance between the first and the last
   man does not increase.
3) Even after exiting, the base endeavors to stay as
   close to the last man as possible.

Championship teams take full advantage of the exist-
ing rules on exiting. Team members position themselves
like pieces of a jigsaw puzzle...contorting, bending, stoop-
ing, squatting, perching or whatevering to make the distance between the first and last man as short as possible. If
you're comfortable in the lineup you are probably slow.
Your position may be so bizarre the only thing that gets
you out the door is the push of those behind you.

There's a big difference between what constitutes the
best exit for you personally and what gives the entire team
the best or fastest exit. It's the team effort that counts and
if you are uncomfortable, that's just too bad. Your job as a
team member is to make a superhuman effort to get the
last man out FAST.

Of course small, low-profile gear helps to tighten up
an exit. It can make a real difference when team scores get
within tenths of seconds of each other.

After your group has figured out and practiced the exit
lineup both with and without gear, you must convert this
static exit position into a dynamic, electric, simultaneous
launch of the entire team into space. A coordinated launch
is effected by a proper verbal countdown.

The countdown leader must have perfect, constant
cadence. His rhythm mustn't vary. He starts the count and

conducts it like a choirmaster. Everyone counts LOUD! Everyone sways together with each beat. On "GO!!" everybody moves. You don't wait for the guy in front of you to move, you move NOW!

Even on fun "garbage" or pick-up loads, it's extremely worthwhile to run through a couple of practice exits. There may be some sky-god who feels he doesn't need the practice, but remind him that the jump is costing *everyone* money and that you need his cooperation and expert guidance on a couple of practice exits. (You smooth talker, you!)

When jumping a small-door aircraft, *stay low* as you dash for the door so you won't have to bend when you reach it. Take short, quick shuffling duck-walk steps. Keep your hands and body on the man in front of you. Dive *before* you get to the door.

If you do it right, you'll find your face touching the backs of the legs of the man in front of you. If you're any further away than that, then you're just not exiting properly. Some people like to hold onto diagonal or leg straps of the person in front of them to ensure there will be no gap as they leave together. Don't worry about causing him or her to go unstable...it can't possibly happen with a forceful enough exit. But be very careful not to push that individual *into* the door frame if you are lunging forward from behind him at an angle.

Exit and the Relative Wind

On exit, your aircraft will have an indicated airspeed of between 80 and 120 miles per hour. When you leave the door, it is this aircraft-generated wind, not the wind produced by your downward fall, on which you do your first few seconds of sub-terminal RW. It's like traveling down the highway in an automobile and holding your arm out the window. You'll feel a strong wind coming from the direction in which the car is traveling—this is the Relative Wind.

Remember this Relative Wind on every exit; use it to your advantage. Let it help you fly toward the star.

How you use the Relative Wind will depend on when you exit the aircraft. If you exit first or second, as part of the base, you must glide or body-surf along with it. You want to keep traveling with the airplane so that when the last men exit, they don't have too far to go to reach you.

If you exit first as a floater, again you must body-surf along with the airplane, tracking on the Relative Wind, so you can catch up with the base-pin men following you.

If you exit in the last half of the load you must execute a strong full flare against the Relative Wind so that you are not carried along with the airplane. You are trying to slow down as quickly as possible so you can begin to work on the star which is behind the aircraft.

If you simply exited and tracked for the star right away, you would actually move away from it until your aircraft-generated speed dissipated itself. Only after that would your track begin to take effect and you would start to move toward the star.

If you can exit with a brief full flare against the Relative Wind of exit, you will pick up 50 to 75 feet toward the star versus a jumper who only exits and waits for his track to take effect.

Depending on the speed of the exit and type of aircraft, the third and fourth men must stay high above the base-pin and thus be able to compensate for any turns, shifts or bobbles they may make. Whether they must flare or surf depends on what happens to the base and how fast the pin is made.

Practical Application of Exit Technique
Do each step of the exit in proper order. Don't antici-pate the next step; concentrate instead on doing each segment to the best of your ability.

First, get into position and visually check that you're properly set to go. Second, calm and clear your mind for the exit. Take a deep breath and exhale slowly; feel your energy build. On the countdown, count out loud! Concen-trate one-pointedly upon the rhythm, cadence and energy buildup of the countdown.

Third, on "GO!!!" get your body moving immediately, releasing energy into a controlled plunge down the hall. Stay low and do not make unnecessary movements. Keep your hands and body on the man in front of you, move with him as a unit. Everyone in the line should move as a chorus line of dancers, or a football lineup.

Fourth, launch yourself toward the door and dive out. Fifth, find the Relative Wind of exit and use it properly. Sixth, start moving into your descent-dive or whatever approach you are using.

But do each of these things separately and perfectly. It will seem disjointed at first, but practice will smooth it out after several jumps. Speed comes only with proper practice and not from simply trying harder. Exit skill goes hand in hand with ability, and ability comes with practice and concentration on each part of the exit.

8-Donut Flake.   *Rande Deluca.*

Chapter VIII
Equipment for Relative Work

 Back when I was jumping in Texas, more than 10 years ago, my favorite jumpwear was a skin-tight pair of coveralls. I liked 'em to fit tight 'cause they looked better—more tailored, y'know. On really hot days I usually opted for cut-off blue jeans, a T-shirt and cowboy boots.

My reserve was mounted real high 'cause that's where the U.S. Army Parachute Team wore theirs. My surplus B-4 harness and backpack were adjusted to their largest size because that's where they slipped eventually anyway. Mainly I didn't care how anything fit. Relative work was called "fun jumping" then, and all my group did was "fun jump." Accuracy was something you did when there was a parachute meet, so we made accuracy jumps at meets and fun jumped otherwise.

My rig fit so loosely it would slip off my shoulders and lie around me in a pile as the C-195 climbed to altitude. So tight was the tailoring on my jumpsuit that I commonly flew in a full spread. I thought I was hot stuff. I could exit fifth at 7200 ft. and get in third by 1500 ft. That was considered to be good.

What took me so long to get in, besides the fact that *nobody* could *do* RW then (except about nine guys in California,) was a lot more than just my poor technique. About seven years later part of the reason finally sunk in ...YOUR PARACHUTE GEAR IS PART OF THE AIRPLANE THAT IS YOUR BODY!!!!!

Fantastic! Gear *does* make a difference! If you arrange your jumpsuit and equipment in an optimum configuration, you can be more effective and efficient at relative work. But what is the optimum? I don't know for sure, but I've been a member of the conference-level champion

4-man team for three years; placed as high as 4th and 5th in both 10-man and 4-man national championship competition; entered a lot of RW meets, and mainly talked to a lot of other RW jumpers. I've also watched people at meets to see what the winners wear and how. I'd like to share my thoughts and ideas on what is the optimum equipment and arrangement for RW with you.

General Notes on Equipment

First, some overall observations on the elements of gear:

Jumpsuit .. made to measure for you, fits well; with bells and plenty big (lots of underarm "wing" area.)

Rig ... snug-fitting harness system that doesn't weigh over 35 lbs. *total* (including containers and canopies.)

Main canopy ... one that lets you down easy and is light and maneuverable; packs up small.

Reserve ... reliable and light.

Main container ... vest-type, no stiffeners. Shape determined by deployment system; lightweight, with a low profile for exit lineup.

Reserve container ... piggyback, or if front-mounted, use the Pop-Top or one of the new wedge-shaped ones.

Pilot chute ... big.

Boots/Shoes ... Adidas tennis shoes, Puma pole vaulting boots, Indian moccasins (wrap-type) or other lightweight, feel-your-feet coverings.

Gloves ... thin (racing driver's) or none.

Helmet ... one that doesn't get in the way. Wear a soft one (a W.W.II leather flying helmet or the like) or a semi-rigid one (French). Or if you can't give up the hard-shell helmet, cut one inch off around the face area of yours and replace the rubber molding. You have to be able to SEE and FEEL!

Goggles ... some that allow good vision. Portias, jockey goggles and "boogie" glasses okay. What we need is an optically-clear Portia-type.

Several companies are now making main canopies that are light and pack up small like a reserve, yet let you down at 12 to 16 feet per second and aren't scary. Some relative workers are jumping 28 ft. Double L's and 7-TU's as well. A few of them use a 4-line release for opening reliability.

Piggyback or tandem systems seem to be a tad faster for momentum RW and post-terminal RW. The mini-pigs aren't much different than conventional gear in terms of "feel" at sub-terminal RW, according to taller relative workers (5'9" and over,) but they help a lot in tight exit lineups.

Some custom-made pig-gear is so small and light the entire rig is lighter, thinner and shorter than a conventional main canopy/harness/container. My pig, for example, totals 34 lbs. and is thinner and only a couple of inches taller than a Super Pro backpack! Part of the secret is a smaller bag that is built around the canopy and tailored to fit the backpack perfectly. In my case the canopy is a Para-Commander.

One of the new "wedgies" or the Pop-Top seem to be the best reserve containers for RW'ers who prefer conventional gear. Those who use them report they work fine and don't get in the way in either the exit lineup or the air.

Choosing Gear...Where to Start

Maybe you're a beginner, or a slow learner, and are considered unskilled. Or to put it another way, maybe you can't enter third on a three-man star 90 per cent of the time. To get better, start with your rig: the container/harness system. Getting a baggy bell-bottom jumpsuit to learn in can be like learning to drive an automobile by practicing in a fuel-dragster or a Formula I race car... scary!

Altering your rig, or buying one that fits your particular needs, requires some thought. How do you fall? ... fast? ... slow? In what position are your arms and legs when you close on the star? Do you have to tuck up ... or spread out ... a lot? Do you find yourself flying with your arms outstretched above your head? Do you always float in the star, or are you usually low in the star? Think about it! Ask people.

Fig. 28. Center of Gravity.

Your center of gravity is just below your navel, in a line intersecting your hip bones. Lay across a bar and stiffen into a full spread to find it. When you fly, fly with your stomach, not your head or "the seat of your pants".

Once you get answers to these questions, write 'em down. Think about them in relation to the center of gravity of your body.

Roughly calculate how wearing your rig the way you do *now* adversely effects your relative work. In a "normal" flight position you should be relaxed and RW Stable. You should not have to keep your hands outstretched, or your legs tucked in, or anything else strange.

Probably the most common conventional rig positioning mistake is wearing the reserve and backpack too high, as style competitors do. This throws your center of gravity toward your head, making your legs float and keeping you flying with your arms outstretched.

Your relative work in this position is slower than it should be. You'll have trouble entering the star because your ass will always want to float. When you get low it's hard to recover altitude unless you're light. And worst of all, you're spending a lot of wasted energy counteracting a misplaced, mispositioned rig! Remember, your gear should detract as little as possible from your flying. Lowering your rig if you wear it too high will certainly help.

The type of equipment you choose isn't really critical. It doesn't matter who made the gear you have. It's like tennis or golf. The racquet or golf clubs don't matter all that much ... it's the person using them and how they are used that counts. Some of the best flyers in the world use old surplus equipment.

If you do want to get new RW gear, get something MADE FOR RW. A lot of the gear on the market today is designed for the stylist. Some of it is unreasonably heavy and bulky. Some brand name manufacturers turn out shoddy merchandise. So look around before you buy. You may find that custom gear in your area is better than anything you can buy over the counter. Whatever you get, make sure it's small and lightweight.

Jumpsuit, Helmet, Boots and Accessories

Members of champion calibre RW teams wear big, baggy, bell-bottomed jumpsuits with lots of excess underarm "wing" material. These jumpsuits are custom-made and cost about $75 to $100+ each. Proper measurement is a must for good fit. Your mass to size ratio should be considered when making your order. A 150 lb. six-footer would want a different amount of material in his jumpsuit than a 200-lb.'er of the same height.

Before deciding to get such a jumpsuit, you should have all the rest of your equipment squared away and fitting properly so they offer the least hinderance to your RW flying. I believe you should also be already somewhat skilled at RW and have all the basics down pat. If you can't enter third after exiting third from 7200 ft. 85 to 90 per cent of the time you should spend the money a custom jumpsuit would cost you on learning RW. You can make quite a few practice jumps for $80.

Putting an oversized jumpsuit on an inexperienced relative worker is foolish. Every movement tends to be exaggerated, and floating becomes a considerable problem for many. Big jumpsuits are for experienced flyers. An exception, of course, is for the fireplug ... extra heavy types who tend to go below any RW group, even in a full spread. These flying bowling balls should get a big-bell jumpsuit right away.

So, if you can never recover lost altitude once you go below, and are sure your recovery reverse arch is proper, then you must get a big jumpsuit just to do normal RW. But I see altogether too many novice hotshots, wearing full-bore RW gear, who zip all over the sky and never get into the formation. They'll always have a good reason like: "No, I couldn't get in but I sure went fast! I burned three guys out the door!"

Concerning boots ... I have never seen any good evidence that the expensive, heavy, cumbersome "French" jump boots offer more protection to the experienced RW'er than a good pair of Adidas or Puma tennis shoes. Importantly, a lighter, thinner shoe helps your feet feel the air. Your feet are just as important as your hands in relative work. If you want to take full advantage of your feet, then the best footwear is tennis shoes with no socks (weather permitting, of course.)

Another good solution is the moccasin-type boot, often called an apres' jump shoe. These make you feel like you have hands on your feet. They do make landings trickier, but if you handle your canopy well and the drop-zone is somewhat flat and clear, you may find moccasins very worthwhile if only for a few jumps. You'll be surprised how much your feet can learn in only five jumps!

The best answer to gloves is to wear none. Or if you wish, wear racing driver's type with a good gripping surface. Again, the goal is to be able to feel the Relative Wind and to use it effectively. Thick gloves often make entries difficult. In the winter, use good quality ski gloves with lots of "feel."

Wear the lightest helmet you can find. Thick, heavy helmets designed for auto racing and motorcycling are an unnecessary burden to the experienced relative worker. Your head is a sensitive judge of the Relative Wind. I think that these helmets are good: cloth or leather ski or flying type, the flexible French "instructors" helmet, and ice hockey and mountain-climbing half-helmets. These are a lot lighter and less cumbersome than a full racing helmet which adds too much weight and restricts your vision.

Goggles present the same problem. Almost every kind on the market badly restrict your side vision. The French portia goggles work well but are terribly blurry and distorted. "Jockey" goggles or "boogie" goggles work better. What would be ideal is an optically clear portia type. People who wear eyeglasses find they can strap them on and that they serve as fairly good goggles. So do wraparound sunglasses.

It is helpful if someone on the load wears an altimeter ... and uses it.

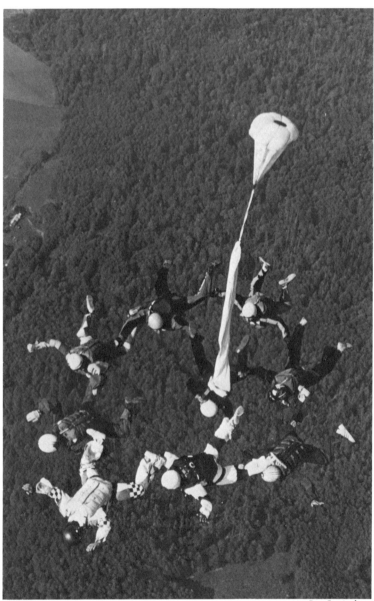

Pull-out from a 9-Diamond.   *Ray Cottingham.*

Chapter IX
Assigned Slots: Pattern Flying and the Quadrant System

 Being at a specific place within a limited amount of time is an integral part of all relative work. When there are several people involved and available time is at a premium, traffic becomes a problem. If ten people exit and track for the same contact point on the star, the result is called "chaotic" and the formation usually ends in a funnel.

It's common, even now, to see some star loads, particularly large-star attempts, where 90 per cent of the people are attempting to enter 30 per cent of available slots—those that are on the closest side of the star. That one side loads up and builds too fast, making the star impossible to fly. In this case, even those few who may have flown around to the back side of the star are hampered, because the mob on the other side is usually pushing, floating or otherwise messing up the star so that it is anything but stable.

A star which is building too fast on one side will usually begin to slide across the sky at alarming speed. Sometimes it moves so fast it "eats" unwary would-be entrants. This gives rise to the old saw, "It slid right under me, honest!"...an excuse that is usually indigestible to all of those on the crowded side who were "waiting their turn to enter."

This traffic jamming also puts a lot of strain on the star, frequently resulting in a dropped grip.

Once upon a time, someone plucked their head out of the nether region and correctly surmised that if the star were imagined to be a clock face, then each flyer could be assigned a particular slot...say, two o'clock, or four o'clock, six, nine, etc. Or the star could be divided into quadrants like a compass, and everyone would have their specific quadrant, say, "northwest."

This did help to eliminate traffic but it created another problem...befuddlement. Many people are lousy at telling left from right, or can't remember where 12 o'clock is in freefall.

Another system, the people and places method, has also been tried. In this system you enter between two pre-assigned people. The word "usually" is key here, because if the star turns or one of the people you're to enter on blows it, you have to improvise.

The method that seems to work best is the fastest and the simplest. It's a combination of assigned slot flying and the quadrant system.

To avoid confusion, any part of the star which is closest to the exit door of the airplane is appropriately called THE *NEAR* SIDE of the star. The other side of the star, the one farthest from the door, is called THE *FAR* SIDE of the star. These near and far sides are further divided into left and right. (If you get confused on left vs. right, just remember that your right hand usually pulls the ripcord; stick the left one in your ear, if you like, unless you're left-handed.)

Now, no matter how the star may turn, you maintain your assigned quadrant and fly the same pattern. For example, if your slot is in the LEFT-NEAR quadrant, you will always exit the plane and fly slightly left and then straight into the left hand part of the near side of the star. If the star should turn, you disregard the turning and still fly the same pattern. The people you enter between may change, but where you enter the star in relation to the airplane is constant. (See Figure 29.)

In assigning slots, take into consideration how each person flies. Some people are much faster using a straight-in approach. They will work best on the near side of the star. Other people like to use a "catch up turn" or back-door entry. They should go to the far side.

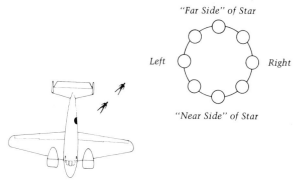

"Far Side" of Star

Left   Right

"Near Side" of Star

Fig. 29. Quadrant System.

Importantly, you should probably have the 9th and 10th men fly to the near side for speed stars since it affords them a direct line, straight-in shot for the fastest time. In this case, 7th and 8th will go to the far side (left and right). Since this is a longer flying distance, you might consider putting your fastest people here.

Two example exit orders might be: first, an ordinary lineup.

Fig. 30.

Exit Order	Position	Slot	
1st	base	NA	rotate base 90° to give #3
2nd	pin	near side	a straight-in shot
3rd	3	near side	
4th	4	far side	
5th	5	near/right	
6th	6	near/left	
7th	7	far/right	
8th	8	far/left	
9th	9	near/right	
10th	10	near/left	

Or, if you use floaters:

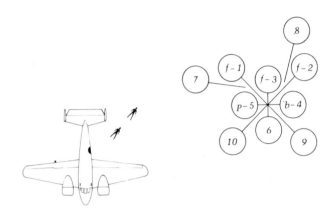

Fig. 31.

Exit Order	Position	Slot	
1st	floater-1	far/left	
2nd	floater-2	far/right	
3rd	floater-3	far	
4th	base	far	
5th	pin	near	
6th	#3	near	
7th	#4	far/left	NOTE: *FLOATERS:*
8th	#5	far right	*don't rush it,*
9th	#6	near/right	*let #3 stable out*
10th	#7	near/left	*the base.*

It is important to note in Figures 30 and 31 that the direction in which the base turns in order to face the oncoming pin will determine the relative positions of the base-pin combo. But, *whichever* way the base does turn, the others still fly their quadrants and patterns as assigned.

Most base-men turn to their right on exiting, though some turn to their left. Turning right is said to be more natural and easier. Turning left is said to be harder but keeps the base-pin closer to the airplane.

Chapter X
Precision Freefall Team Relative Work Maneuvers and Sequential Plays

 The visual exultation of seeing fine precision relative work flying on film is surpassed only by the joy of being part of the jump yourself. With precise control you fly an individual RW dance that intertwines and connects with others in geometric shapes, and then, perhaps, sequences into yet another maneuver. It fills your heart and soul with exhilaration. It's legal!

Fantastic figures in billowy rainbows of colored gear swoop like a Phoenix on the living pattern as it builds in a slow motion, coordinated dance on the uprushing air. Each flyer seems to be performing his own ballet in beautiful unity with the others.

Perhaps you dress in stunning brilliances of color which your freefall brothers can add to the technicolorful, three-dimensional movie they are watching, as their imaginations collectively ebb and flow into the completed maneuver.

Think of the blinding blue of two miles high, and the duller patchwork of earth that frames the flying pattern. Only an occasional flashing cloud notices the masterpiece till it explodes in a rocket burst ending in flowering canopies. If only film could also capture the 500,000-watt energy flow, and the thundering symphony of sound..."Roll-over, Beethoven—tell Tchaikovsky the news!"

A good fast exit and speed are required in all forms of relative work. In competition speed stars, speed and skill in the exit, descent, flare, and docking/entry maneuvers are vital. In good speed stars, all flying is classified as momentum RW. Flyers maintain the momentum of their descent/track and redirect it to enter the star, without ever stopping. In good sequential relative work, flying is classified as both momentum and non-momentum RW. Flyers maintain the momentum of the descent/track and carefully redirect it to fill their slot. Then the entire formation may transition into non-momentum RW to build a sequential maneuver(s).

Both speed-star and sequential RW require a good exit. And in both, the base is key.

While most people like any kind of RW, some people like one type better than another. Neither is superior nor inferior to the other. It depends on what you like to do. Some prefer sequential or alternate maneuver flying because it's more immediately fun than all the concentrated team jumps you have to make to be good at 10-man speed stars.

Alternate maneuvers and sequential "plays" do require more flying from all the people on the team. Everyone is assigned a particular slot and plays are run as in football. No one can be late for their slot, or get low, because there are other people waiting for him to fill his position before they can take theirs. Diagrams of the plays are usually required, often filed in a team's "playbook."

Since the plays themselves are hard to visualize, even on paper, you have to do a lot of ground practice for successful sequential RW. When you begin, start small (four to six people) and build up. A lot of the maneuvers that seem complex are simply constructed from smaller segments. Practice these four to six-person segments to learn how to "helicopter," to fly backwards, and to switch grips. Grip switching gives symmetry to the sequence from maneuver to maneuver.

The "switch signal" system is key. The last man in shakes his grip and it is telegraphed around the pattern. The runners drop their grips and helicopter to the next contact area, while grips are switched throughout the pattern until the next maneuver is completed.

You'll find that loads of either four, ten, 16 or 20 are best for symmetrical plays and sequential maneuvers.

As the first maneuver in a sequential RW skydive builds, precision is critical. You must dock at your assigned position so as to have no effect on the building maneuver's stability. Others wait to enter, or await your entry, to settle in and help fly the pattern to completion.

When you're in a maneuver like a French Connection, a Wedge or a Tripod, you may be somewhat visually isolated from the center of the figure. Because of this, you must pay particular attention to your relative flying so that your position and flying attitude do not give unwanted movement to the whole pattern. Watch the ground. Watch the other flyers in the pattern. Feel your attitude.

When you get the switch signal, act immediately. In unison with the others, fly to your next contact area. Fast non-momentum RW requires full use of your body. Get into it. Gain a bit of altitude while you hand-track. Drop/glide/helicopter into your next slot...you may even be called on to fly backwards! Fly it!

Never expect the pattern to absorb any excess speed you have. Docking shock will snap a ripple through it that may amplify into a wave of self-destruction. Be precise. Put your body where it is supposed to be. Make a no-wrinkle entry. Get a caressing but vise-like grip on your contact man's jumpsuit, or somewhere that won't impede his ability to help fly the maneuver.

If you're on the outer ends, make sure you don't unconsciously turn the maneuver either clockwise or counter-clockwise. Don't float or sink. Be aware. If you fly at the point, or front, be very careful. Have a good sense for where *straight down* is, and use it.

On break-up, turn away from the maneuver and max-track away from its imagined center before you wave off to pull.

The word "play" used in planning alternate maneuver and sequential skydives comes from "football play." Similarities between the two plays are very direct.

In any professional football play, each man on the team has a particular assignment, and the play is not successful unless every man does his assignment well. The timing, symmetry and beautifully coordinated motion of a pro-football play can be so perfect it is awesome. In RW plays, the same is true. Everyone has a particular slot on a particular sequence and the play cannot be successfully completed unless each individual does his job well. As in football, timing and teamwork are critical.

Vertical Tri-Diamond.   *Ray Cottingham.*

Chapter XI
Sport

"Like so much of life, football presents us with the choice of responding either with fear or with action and clarity."

—John Brodie[6]

One day, football star John Brodie got together with Michael Murphy, president of Esalen Institute, to discuss Sport. Not just the physical aspects, but the underlying psychic elements that the uninitiated would call "occult." Their conversation, recorded in *Intellectual Digest*, reveals an aspect of Sport that is particularly applicable to skydiving. Murphy noted that some surfers, skydivers, skiers and football players talk a language that is almost mystical.

John Brodie, quarterback for the San Francisco 49'ers for more than 16 years, knows a lot about ground-team relative work. He is only one step behind Johnny Unitas for the record of yards gained passing in the NFL. He is also a championship golfer.

Michael Murphy is president and co-founder of the Esalen Institute in California, and author of *Golf in the Kingdom*, a metaphysical sports fantasy that explores what Murphy calls the "hidden side of sport."

Both men feel there is a lot to the game that has not been described by all the renowned sportswriters and football analysts. All of these spectators, knowledgeable though they be, are missing something.

Brodie says a great many football players feel the same way about the sport he does:

"There is a side to the game that really hasn't been described yet—that 'hidden' side of sport you talk about in your book, things having to do with the psychological side

---

[6]*Intellectual Digest*, January 1973, p. 19.

of the game, with what we might call 'energy flows,' and the extraordinary states of mind performing athletes sometimes get into."

Everyone injects their own reality into football—a reality that may not mesh with the actuality of the sport. Brodie's reality of the sport includes "energy flows" which he defines:

"Often, in the heat and excitement of a game, a player's perception and coordination will improve dramatically. At times, and with increasing frequency now, I experience a kind of clarity that I've never seen adequately described in a football story. Sometimes, for example, time seems to slow way down, in an uncanny way, as if everyone were moving in slow motion. It seems as if I have all the time in the world to watch the receivers run their patterns, and yet I know the defensive line is coming at me just as fast as ever. I know perfectly well how hard and fast those guys are coming and yet the whole thing seems like a movie or a dance in slow motion. It's beautiful."

What he is describing, as the Yaqui Indian sorcerer, Don Juan, points out to Carlos Castaneda in *A Yaqui Way of Knowledge*, is that you see more clearly because you are a warrior in a state which can only be defined as "non-ordinary reality."

In *Golf in the Kingdom*, Murphy discusses "energy streamers" that a golf ball rides on its way toward the hole—lines of force that seem to emanate from the golfer when he can visualize and execute his shot in a moment of high clarity.

I often experience this phenomena while skydiving. And it used to occur during fencing and racing when I engaged in those sports. My personal approach to doing relative work is predicated, in part, on this theory. Strangely, perhaps, the other part is imagined music—a classical symphony written to the roar of the airplane and the rush of the wind. Plus a beautiful vision of dancers performing an ecstatic ballet choreographed by the clouds.

All body movement, as martial arts masters state, is directed by energy flows which emanate from the area of the stomach. This idea is further substantiated by the Yogin who says the stomach is one of the principal power centers. So, you fly with your stomach as much as your head.

Yes, it sounds bizarre. But can it be learned? Can you practice and develop clarity during a relative work jump? Can you strengthen your intentions? As John Brodie says,

"Yes. Pressures that used to get me down don't affect me to the same extent now. I've learned to shed certain destructive attitudes when a game is under way. A player's effectiveness is directly related to his ability to be right there, doing that thing, in the moment. All the preparation he may have put into the game—all the game plans, analysis of movies, etc.—is no good if he can't put it into action when game time comes. He can't be worrying about the past or the future or the crowd or some other extraneous event. He must be able to respond in the here and now. This is an ability we all have potentially. I believe it is our natural state. But because most of us lose it as we grow up, we have to regain it."

Agreed, it does sound like Zen or a similar spiritual discipline. These same ideas, phrased differently, appear in the *Bhagavad-Gita*, in at least seven separate Buddhist texts (see translations by E. Y. Evans-Wentz), and also in the *Tao Te Ching* and elsewhere in Eastern religious philosophy.

As Michael Murphy said:

"It seems to me that in many ways sport is like a Western Yoga. I have heard mountain climbers, surfers, sky divers and skiers who talk a language that is almost mystical, and now I hear you talking the same way.

Brodie: Call it mystical if you like. For me it is simply one of the elementary facts of experience. Here-and-now awareness, clarity, strong intention, a person's "tone level"—these are things a lot of people who don't know anything about Yoga or mysticism talk about. The trouble is, people don't make them operative in their life as often as they could.

Murphy: But some of the things you seem to suggest, like a ball jumping over a defender's hands or time slowing down, go beyond ordinary experience. In the East, and in our Western religious traditions, there have been disciplines to develop these extraordinary powers and states of mind. But the modern Western world, for the most part, is lacking in such disciplines. They seem esoteric and alien to most of us. Maybe that is one of the reasons sportswriters and sports commentators find it difficult to comprehend the kinds of things you are talking about."

It's not surprising that people find it difficult to grasp these ideas. One of the problems is language:

"**Murphy:** One of the problems coaches and players have—and it's a problem all of us have in talking about these things—is that our language about unusual powers and states of mind is so limited. We don't have commonly understood words to describe "energy flows" or what you call "being clear." These expressions don't make sense to a lot of people. I think the time has come to begin creating a language and an understanding about these dimensions of life.

Brodie: Athletics could be a place where this kind of insight is developed. Sport is one of the few activities in which many Americans spend a great deal of time developing their potentialities. It influences character, I think, as much as our schools and churches do. But, even so, it falls far below what it could be. It leaves out so much. I would love to see a sports team developed with a more fulfilling purpose."

Try it. Many four-man RW teams and ten-man RW teams do have a special kind of communication in freefall. We read each other so well that we know where we need to be in a given situation. We make contact somewhere in the field of our existence, amidst all the flux and within all the sound and fury of the rushing sky. It's a highly intuitive thing. It's our thing, for there's a kind of communication, a kind of *being* if you will, that happens during an inspired jump.

And, after a jump is a lot like after a game. Brodie

mentions a statement made by Alan Page, defensive tackle for the Minnesota Vikings and NFL most valuable player for 1971. Page described his feelings of comedown after a game is over. He said it was a weird feeling adjusting back to ordinary reality, to sanity, to having to be a person again.

I know what he means. Life can be like a soap opera after a good jump. You can get into a different order of reality when you're doing RW, a non-ordinary reality that just doesn't mesh with the black-and-white-with-no-gray lines that many people use to delineate life.

When you make an RW jump, when you line up for the exit, you are tuning into the situation. You clear yourself by dropping useless emotional buildup and other distractions. Your goal is to be focused and sensitive. Don't worry about results. That's later, and later never exists.

"Relative work done with anxiety about results is far inferior to relative work done without such anxiety. In the calm of controlled abandon, seek refuge in the knowledge of the art of relative work. Those who work selfishly for results are miserable."

Adapted from the BHAGAVAD-GITA,
"Song of God"

★ ★

Brodie explains his perception of knowledge:

"Brodie: I equate creativity with awareness. It's a matter of simple knowledge. The more I know, the more I can do.

Murphy: But knowing like this is more than the kind of knowing we are supposed to learn in school, more than verbal knowing or book knowing. It involves a tuning in to subtle energies and feelings and forces we can only come to through direct awareness. It involves the emotions and the spirit as well as the intellect—and the here and now, the complexities and subtleties of a given situation rather than preconceptions about it, or your rehearsals of it or what has been written in a book about it. It seems to me that this sort of knowing leads to a new kind of being.

Murphy: After hearing you talk I gather that top athletes are people who are accustomed to altering time, who are accustomed to a higher state of focus and concentration, who are accustomed to altered perceptions of many types and to going with the inner flow of things. But I don't see any of this on the sport pages. Or in the sport books you hear about, or on the radio and TV programs. Our culture seems to screen it all out, even though such experience is at the very heart of a game so many of us love.

Brodie: That's right. It's a case of experience being ahead of what we can say about it. Maybe if we could talk about it more clearly we could make it happen more. Sport is so important in creating values in America, it would be great if it could open up these inner dimensions for people. It's really what many coaches and players want to do, after all. They want sport to be more than winning at any cost, more than beating people up and making money and getting ahead over somebody else's dead body. But we have got to break out of this conspiracy to belittle sport and human nature."

And most fittingly, I think, this champion of the American sport concludes:

"It is better to improve the game, I think, than to indulge in a lot of idle criticism of it. And when you look at its history you see that it has already gone through enormous changes. It is a much different game than it was in the 1920s or 30s. It's a more complex and artistic game now, with all the offensive and defensive plays, with the game plans and the variety of skills involved. Why shouldn't the game go on changing? I see no reason why we should fix the game of football where it is, after the change it has gone through already. Why shouldn't it be a place to develop the mental and spiritual dimensions we have been talking about?"

★   ★   ★

"By letting it go it all gets done.
The world is won by those who let it go.
But when you try and try,
The world is then beyond winning."

                                    –Tao Te Ching

Double Horizontal Opposed Diamonds.

8-Bipole Flake.

8-Donut.   *Sequential series by Ray Cottingham.*

Chapter XII
Relative Work Competition and Team Organization

Competition is an integral part of our way of life. Survival itself might be called competition with the elements. Certainly our Judeo-Christian work ethic, or the Puritan work ethic, if you will, proclaims that those who work hard will receive greater rewards than those who don't. Competition is fostered by the institutions of our society: schools, the military, the family and organizations of all types for all age groups.

Many philosophers believe that competition—the desire to excel—is one of man's basic needs. Robert Ardrey, for example, author of *African Genesis* and *The Territorial Imperative*, believes that the carving out of a personal niche, accompanied by the drive to fight for it, is more basic than any other drive, including sex.

"**Competition:** a rivalry, contest, match. ... (SYN) denotes a striving for the same object, position, prize, etc., usually in accordance with certain fixed rules." —*Webster's New World Dictionary of the American Language*[7]

Most definitions of the word "competition" center around the Ego and relate to aggrandizement of same. Many people see competition only as a quest for personal glory. The quest to "be the best," or "Number One." ... "Winning isn't everything, it's the ONLY thing" ... and "Nothing counts except first place" ... I'm sure you know many more of these brash saws.

Some relative workers pursue competition from this point of view. Others approach it a bit differently—as a chance to do the thing they really like to do with teammates with whom they feel in harmony.

[7] College Edition, 1966.

Organized RW competition provides a setting for both approaches. At the site of a meet there are many others who share your interest. It's a fun, social setting. You pay your jump money plus extra to provide toilets, trophies, extra aircraft, and profit for the hard-working organizers.

All you have to do is relax and wait for your load to be called. Then you go up and do your thing with your team. It's what you've been practicing for months. You try to do as well as you've done in practice ... as well as you've been doing over the last several jumps. You do not try to go faster. (The try-to-go-faster part was something you experimented with in practice prior to the meet.) You assume that you'll do at least as well as you usually do. Except that it's more fun because there's the electricity of a team working together, each member giving his all to win the event.

It's the same feeling you would get if you were driving a really fast car in a race, or giving your all in a high-jump event. You are a highly trained athlete, in good condition and peak form. And you're doing that which you most love to do, and that is to fly.

Types of RW Competition

There are two freefall relative work competition events recognized by the Federation Aeronautique Internationale, which makes the rules for international competition. They are the 10-man star event and the four-man sequential event. The U.S.P.A. National Parachuting Championships are held to recognize national and conference parachuting champions in four-man and ten-man team relative work performance, and "to select the top parachutists within the United States to compose a representative United States Parachute Team for participation in selected international parachuting competitions."[8]

Advantages of Being on a Team

When you jump with a team it can be a wonderful experience. You don't have to scrounge around and dredge

[8]U.S.P.A., Part 50, Competition Rules and Regulations.

up people to jump with. The team captain or manager does all the manifesting for you. You tend to get more jumps with a team because the team has collective snivel power. The manifestor knows you want to jump, that you have a load together, and that you'll get your lift off as soon as you can. That keeps the airplanes running and you jumping.

You can also learn a lot about precision RW while jumping with a team. By jumping in the same position and with the same people every time, you'll learn more about how are you flying in relation to others. They'll be a constant against which you can practice the art of flying your body. Additionally, after a while the team can accomplish esoteric RW maneuvers that probably couldn't be completed by jumpers who didn't know the steady consistency of a team and the confidence of knowing ... of being *certain* that the situation will be as planned when you arrive at your slot.

And, you get a lot of star time. Star time is that time which you spend flying *in* a star. On non-team loads you tend to spend most of the time exiting, tracking, correcting for a moving base, entering the star, and very little time flying as part of that star.

Getting star time is invaluable because it teaches you how to do contact relative work ... a very advanced type of RW in which you fly in concert with the others locked into the formation. You learn to react relative to those who are also reacting to a changing formation. The end result is a very stable formation.

A star with just a few people in it who are really heads up on star flying can make a world of difference between what gets entered in the logbook as a completed maneuver and what gets entered as an attempt. So when you're on a team, you'll be in more *completed* maneuvers. That's a nice feeling.

Then, too, there's status connected with jumping with a team. It means you're a competition RW flyer. You've shown yourself to be good enough, or at least to have the enthusiasm and stamina, to be "part of the team."

Before takeoff you don't need to drag everyone together for the load. You'll meet for ground practice before every jump. You'll practice exits with people who will really put their hearts into it because they all recognize how important the exit is to the team. Hopefully there will be no loafing, or sluggish laggards, on your team.

There's less of that old "let's just go up and see what we get" attitude. You have an assigned seat in the plane—your ticket is collected.

On jump-run the exit lineup will build professionally as the star-master spots. The exit countdown, being well rehearsed before each jump, actually helps your exit. You know the motion and sway of the lineup by heart, and you can dash to the door in cadence to get a good shotgun exit for everyone.

Outside the airplane you'll know where the star is and what your flight pattern is to be. You can then concentrate on perfecting your flying. You're familiar with the falling speed of the star so your flare-point requires less guesswork. After entry you fly in coordination with your mates. And you'll feel the electric charge of good vibes that flows through a team when it's a good jump. It's exhilarating.

At break-off time there's less worry about a midair collision or canopy pass. Back on the ground there'll be a critique of the jump that lets you know what went on and gives you an idea how and where you can improve on your next jump.

And in competition you'll have the joy and pride of pitting your hard-earned skill against others with the same interests. It can be a very rewarding experience.

How to Be a Good Team Member

The commitment required of every member of a competition relative work team is essential to the well-being and success of the team. Each member should be willing to stand before his teammates and agree to the extent of the commitment as outlined by the captain. Without full agreement among all members as to just what you are trying to do, and when and how it'll be done, you will be sowing seeds of misunderstanding that may grow into bitterness later. Don't make any assumptions. Talk it over thoroughly.

Here's a partial list of things that must be agreed to, and once agreed to, adhered to:

1. You will be available for every team practice, without exception.
2. Team practice will officially start at a certain time and day each weekend.
3. You will be present, without exception, at or before that time.
4. You will have all your gear ready to jump at that time.
5. You will be awake and alert when you appear at practice. You will announce your presence to the captain or team manager. You will be ready to put your gear on.
6. You will be a positive contributor to the team meeting.
7. You will participate in ground practice and practice exits to the best of your ability.
8. You will suit up promptly when the load is called.
9. You will have your jump ticket ready.
10. You will be considerate of your team members, and of course, you'll make your best effort on the jump.

After the jump:

1. You will attend the team meeting or pack promptly as requested.
2. If you have any angry tirades, you will keep them to yourself.
3. If you have legitimate complaints or constructive criticisms, you will pass them on quietly, tactfully and privately, if possible, to the team captain. He will handle them as he deems appropriate.
4. You will be ready for the next jump. Never keep your teammates waiting.

You should not display uncontrolled hostility or anger, because it accomplishes nothing except to put a strain on everyone. Team jumping is very trying and may be hard on your nerves. Realize this and watch for it. Remember the positive reasons you are jumping with the team.

Unjumpable weather bums out everyone. Tensions and bad feelings are harder than ever to control. If a team splits up, or has a divorce, it's often during a long spell of bad weather.

"Do Not Feed the Judges"

Judging relative work is a difficult task—and an art all its own. Judging requires a quickness of eye and extreme patience that few people possess. RW judges who are good at it will record their respective times to within three-tenths of a second of one another.

If RW competition is to continue to improve, the critical element of judging cannot be overlooked. Serious teams should develop their own training judges. This will give the team a constant source for ground timers during practice so that progress can be evaluated. Importantly, it will also provide a judge for meets who has trained as hard as the competitors themselves. The result will be better meets and more accurate judging.

The serious team should have a team fund. One of the first acquisitions should be a good quality stop watch suitable for judging. An inexpensive cassette tape recorder is also a good judge-team training aid. The recorder is used as the star forms and the judging calls made: "Exit! ... 2,3 ... 4,5 ... 6,7,8,9,10." As the tape is replayed, the team may note slow spots. The judge can re-check his time. Individual team members can keep track of their own personal progress by timing from the tape.

At meets it is important to assist the judges wherever possible. Someone should be sure they get food and drink throughout the day. The judging sites should be separated so that judges cannot hear each other's calls. Judging sites should be made as comfortable as possible, with shade from the sun.

The meet judges are trying to do their best, just as you are. How well they do depends on how well they are equipped and trained. If they're uncomfortable and hot, or can't communicate with the manifestor, meet director and aircraft easily, you can expect problems. Yes, *YOU* can expect problems. If team captains do not check out the judging setup and equipment before the first round starts, it is too late for complaints about bad judging later.

When the meet is underway, remember that you came to jump, not to hassle, complain or protest. Avoid becoming entangled in judging hassles while at a meet. If it is a so-called "fun" meet and the judging and competition is casual, it is unreasonable to complain bitterly if you get what you consider a bad call.

If you want judges who are as good at their thing as you are at yours, you must be willing to help train them and to spend more money to make their time worthwhile. This may mean higher meet entry fees to cover motel rooms, digital timers, tape recorder rental, communications equipment rental, sun shades, etc. But if you've trained hard for the meet, it should be worth it to you.

Your national parachuting organization, U.S.P.A., can often lend a hand. They have telemeters and other judging aids available for loan through Conference directors. But you must inform them, and ask for their assistance.

Team Organization

The team captain is critical to the success of the team. He must have the support of the entire team. After practice times, dates, places, and how many jumps to be made each day are agreed on by the team, the captain must make sure that these stated practice goals are accomplished. He organizes ground practice and establishes team exit order.

Since attitude and enthusiasm are critical in competition RW, the captain should be able to inspire and bring out these traits in his team as well. He is the quarterback. Team members owe him their respect and support. It's a tough job. Give your captain all the consideration you can.

The team can work together much more smoothly if it is well organized. This is not a simple task. Frequently a team will have a team manager in addition to a captain to handle these organizational problems and to help ensure that the team's time is spent effectively. Collecting money for loads, handling team communications are two important jobs that a manager can handle.

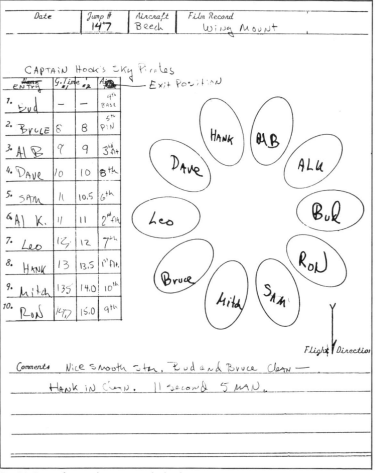

Fig. 32. Example page from a team logbook.

A team logbook is an excellent idea, too. It will show strengths and weak spots in recording progress. It can be compared with the stated team goals. It will give the team an idea of problems that may occur consistently.

As for team exit order, the base-pin combo are two of the key slots on a 10-man team. If the other members are good, they'll look great working on a good base. If you want to build a sub-20 second star, the base-pin needs to be superhuman at subterminal RW. That, plus starmastering and/or spotting, and the importance of their slots for speed put a lot of pressure on these two—so they must be cool under all conditions.

The base man does about 50 or 60 percent of the pinning. He doesn't "just lay there" or backslide, but works toward the pin who is descending on him rapidly. On speed stars this usually means that he glides along with the airplane after exit maintaining its speed so that he and the pin have a minimum of horizontal distance to cover. On really good speed star teams, the base man is an ace.

If you have a fast 10-man team, try putting four of the fastest men out first. Be sure they have good subterminal ability. Going out of a large door airplane requires an *instant* four-man because the "gob" exit puts everyone THERE. The challenge is to enter fast and smooth. To enter at all, you must have an open slot. To have *any* slots you must have an immediate two-man. To build a 15-sec. 10-man you must have a four-man in about seven seconds. If you don't think that is hard, try it.

Avoid forming or joining a team unless you have enough time and money to make a useful addition to the team.

Be sure the goal of the team is understood by everyone. It takes a long, long time to build a championship team. If your goal is limited only to winning—placing first and nothing else—then don't bother. Winning comes from doing good relative work with your teammates, and working with (not against) them. It comes from entering RW meets just for the practice of competition. Winning comes from everyone placing the strength of the team over their own ego.

Join a team to do good RW and to learn to do better RW. Join a team to have some fun along with a lot of work that will be challenging and satisfying. If you insist on "winning or nothing", try the individual events where your ravings won't hinder someone else's efforts.

Chapter XIII
How to Do Four-Man RW

 Four-man relative work is the "official" name for a specified set of maneuvers that has its own event in international competition. It preceded 10-man competition at the national level because historically many small drop zones without large aircraft do have a four-place airplane. Four man RW at many drop zones is also known as fun jumping—often unorganized and usually just messin' around.

Here we want to talk about F.A.I. international four-man. It is one of the most exacting and artful, yet *fun* relative work swoopin' I've ever done. It really sharpens your skill.

The watch starts in four-man RW when everyone backloops out of the initial four-man star and sequences into one of six specified maneuvers. Completion of the second maneuver is your score.

Four-man differs from 10-man RW not only in number of participants, but in types of flying. After the backloop, four-man RW flying is largely of the "non-momentum" type. You do your backloop and immediately set up to swoop on over and take your place in the next maneuver. You feel a lot like an eagle, whether you're closing the tail of a diamond in about six seconds, or becoming the point man for a fast caterpillar. It'll give you the same thrill and sense of professional excitement that setting a good car into a four-wheeled drift and powering it out does.

What It's Like

You try to relax as the cut is given and you climb out to your spot on the strut, hanging on to wait while everybody else clambers out. It seems to take forever. Then on "READY ... 2 ... 1 ... GO!" you float away into the slow-falling, on-the-edge flying of subterminal RW.

You execute a slow motion dive-turn with your stomach and a turn-flare. All this while you are falling in a thin, tenuous wind that quietly gets stronger. You feel as if you're falling on waxed wires as you dance lightly and carefully into that 4 to 7 second initial four-man star. You dock with a heart-rushing swoop and then, only when everyone is in, do you all break grips into a four-man star.

Now the electricity starts. Each one concentrates on the face of the teammate who will key the backloop. He sing-counts a rhythmic cadence until you've reached full terminal velocity. His brow knits. "Uhm-chugga-la-la! ... GO!"

Bango! You push down on the up-rushing wind and quickly shift into high gear. While still on the down side of your backloop you spot your point man and swing toward him. As you end your backloop you're into a half-flare. Getting big, you spread out and use every part of your body to fly toward that invisible, intuitive spot where all four of you will meet in formation. You may be flying sideways, even backwards if you're the point man.

If you're entering third or fourth into the second maneuver, you'll grab some extra altitude and be headed for your docking point before it happens. You'll be moving fast for the close, aiming for a low time. With a firm grip you fly it authoritatively, watching the point man who at 3500 ft., like an alarm clock, pulls his main.

When you see his pilot chute you'll split into a track before pulling. You'll sit there in the saddle, overwhelmed. Your heart will pump. You'll feel like you just got off a wild ride at the amusement park. Yessir.

Getting Together as a Team—The Commitment

If you want to do some serious, hard-core RW...if you want to have a lot of fun...if you want to pick up a lot of RW technique in a short period of time, then get together with a four-man team. You'll need three others who are into the same thing you are, and then you'll need a solemn commitment from each to:

1. Always be there for practice at the appointed time. Even if it is raining, be there.
2. Agree that during designated practice periods, four-man team jumps come first.
3. Always do at least five practice sessions on the ground before each jump.
4. Participate in a debriefing immediately after each jump, no matter how hot or tired you may be. This is where you figure out what you did, and what you'll do next time to make that maneuver faster.
5. Apply enthusiasm and stick-to-it-ness. Determine to make at least 30 practice jumps.

Your first ten or so jumps as a team may be disheartening. It will seem impossible. But keep at it. Try to think of ways to help the team work better together. Soon it will begin to click.

You don't have to love your teammates. You don't even have to like them, though it helps. You *do* have to like jumping, because four-man RW is a lot of jumping. Four-man RW will make a flyer out of you. The things it teaches you are subtle. You'll find yourself using techniques learned in four-man in sequential and alternate maneuver RW, as well as speed stars.

Home planning sessions are a good place to start getting it all together. Every team member should be provided with a set of the rules (U.S.P.A. Part 50) and pictures of the maneuvers. The captain and hopefully everybody on the team will think about the maneuvers and contribute their ideas on doing them. These ideas all add up to a game plan.

The four-man RW team's game plan need not be written, but will show each man's position and how he should get there for maximum speed. A master team logbook is a definite advantage though not a must.

After the plan for each jump is developed, talk about it. Discuss the details. Try to think in terms of the best team rather than the best "you." Agree on each step of the way.

Ground Practice

Ground practice in relative work can be an effective conditioner for both mind and body when done before every jump. It's helpful on a fun jump but essential for a team practice load.

It may be compared to rugby or football practice or any other team sport where coordinated interaction with one's teammates is required. You learn to work together and coordinate your movements on the ground so that every maneuver becomes reflexive, and the jump will fall together more easily in the air.

It requires many jumps to develop group skill and team attitude, and that is why you must supplement air-work with ground training. All good teams do ground practice. Even if you are planning just a "fun jump" with four or five people, a little run-through on the ground before the jump will quickly point out any traffic problems that may pop up in the air, and will help put everybody's head in the same place.

On the ground, slowly walk through the entire jump at least four times before every load. Have someone count the seconds out loud; listen to the cadence. Build the star (standing) just as you will in the air, starting from the plane. Imagine that you *are* in freefall. Don't build a four-man star in four seconds if you usually take 8 to 10 seconds in actual freefall.

Key off the backloop just as you do in the air. Walk into the next maneuver in proper sequence and in proper timing. Then imagine break-off time and practice pull sequence.

It is a lot easier to learn the various maneuvers of four-man RW on the ground rather than wasting a lot of time in the air. Spend a lot of ground practice learning the mechanical steps. More importantly, spend some time to learn the cadence of the jump so that you all feel every maneuver together. Do each maneuver the same way each time.

The Theory of the Exit

When competition four-man RW was first conceived, not every jump began with a four-man star. There were several specified sequences, i.e. a diamond to a skirmish line or an arrowhead to a snowflake. Teams were timed from the exit to completion of the second maneuver, and exit technique became a very important part of the jump.

A few years ago the event was changed to its present form, all sequences beginning with a star, to strengthen the flying portion of the jump. Scores are now computed from the backloop to the completion of the second maneuver. While Herculean gymnastics on exit are no longer required to cut time, a good, clean, fast exit is really the base for any relative work maneuver, and particularly four-man RW.

The ideal is to exit in such a manner that the four-man is made in less than nine seconds. I consider seven seconds to be average. Anything less than six is impressive and probably unnecessary, unless you just dig it.

A typical four-man exit will see a hanger dangling beneath the wing strut, holding on in the windblast. Next to him is the base facing forward, then the pin facing either forward or backwards as preference dictates. With only one leg and arm in the door, hanging down the side of the plane as far as he can, is the number four man—the first man away.

He is the first man away because he is knocked from his position by the forceful exit of the base/pin. He must turn and float up into the base/pin. The hanger will drop off the strut and slowly dive-turn on the subterminal air to reach the base. Movements in subterminal RW are very slow. However, this allows a high rate of closure in docking.

The base and pin must fight the temptation to hook up instantly. They should wait two or three seconds, keeping eye contact all the while, before linking. The third man docks on wrists and should not enter until the fourth man docks, too. If he breaks into the two-man right away, it may bobble and mess up the fourth man's approach.

Backloop and Second Maneuver

Now the jump speeds up. If you've done a quick four-man you haven't even achieved terminal velocity yet. It may be four to six seconds away. The backloop key-man should take this into account and wait until terminal before starting the countdown for the backloop. It is important to be at terminal velocity for the backloop because it will provide greater control and stability, as stylists are well aware.

On the backloop command, each man does not push away, but releases his grip and does a firm, fast backloop. On the downside, or backside, of the backloop each man starts moving toward the projected area of the sky that will become the contact point of the second maneuver. This is where good timing and a *lot* of ground practice pay off.

Your point man (on whom the second maneuver builds) must have rock-solid nerves. After the backloop he smoothly and quickly executes an on-axis 180° turn, always in the same direction. Then he flies slowly backwards to that point which represents the imaginary "point of least distance" between all four.

His ability to fly backwards slowly and precisely in a fluid, steady way is one of the keys to a fast maneuver. Everyone else is approaching that same spot. Ground practice and timing pay off here, too.

The backloop is a very important part of the jump. If all four team members execute their backloops on heading and without losing position on each other, the second maneuver will fall together much more easily. The fact that relative work backloops teach you to fly upside down is just a side benefit.

Practice backloops with your team in freefall. Practice them in a swimming pool, too. The water slows down the sequence and you become more aware of each movement of the body that you use to accomplish the backloop.

As your backloop is 300 °, or almost complete, survey what has/is happening to your fellow fliers. You may need to use the remaining 60° downside of your backloop to make a dive-turn to the contact area. Snap into a full recovery position and *at the same time,* dip a shoulder or snap a leg toward the contact point.

At the contact point, be absolutely sure your entry angle and docking will assist the entry of another flier in the formation. If you hit so as to push the formation or cause it to warp, it will certainly affect the speed and smoothness with which it is built. Success is communicated by the fourth man in who double shakes legs and arms.

Meanwhile the point man is flying the formation, making sure it does not track forward or backwards or turn. At the same time he is watching the altitude. At 3500 ft. he pulls his main. This is a signal for the other three to do a 180° turn to track away and pull.

It can be dangerous to be close to one another at pull time. If you find yourself close to a teammate at pull time, dive-turn away from him. Wait until he gets line stretch before you pull.

Having the point man pull high relieves many dangers. He is a very critical safety valve and must be relied on never to forget his responsibility. If he pulls consistently at 3500 ft., his teammates need never worry about when it is time to track and pull.

Chapter XIV
For the RW Novice

When you're first starting to do large-star relative work your most fervent desire is to be included on eight-man and larger RW loads. You want to get your SCR and SCS and "do" large-star RW. But getting on a load is often a problem.

Most RW novices grossly overrate their own RW skill. Since the load manifestor doesn't share your ego-blindness, he may not be sympathetic.

Analyze *your* situation—can you come in third or fourth 90 per cent of the time on small star loads? If not, you lack the real qualifications for big star loads where the mental tension you place on yourself will degrade your RW performance to an unacceptable level. A realistic self-assessment of your actual RW proficiency level is the first step to "doing" large-star RW.

Check your log book. Divide your total number of RW jumps into your total number of *successful* RW jumps. The resulting percentage will give you an idea of your skill level. If it's less than 80 per cent, you need practice. That is, RW practice, not large-star RW practice.

Results of a Bad Entry.

Andy Keech.

RW Skill Test

Another RW skill test (which is also excellent practice for RW of any kind) incorporates the following maneuvers. Starting with the easier and progressing to the more difficult you should, on a 30-second delay, be able to:

Jump	Maneuver	Proficiency Recommended
1	Make contact with a novice who is already making controlled 30-second delays. Novices are hard to catch, since their RW skill is low.	90%
2	Make a two-man hookup with another RW novice; then separate and do a 360° turn, another hookup; repeat. Make three separate hookups from 7200 ft.	80%
3	2-man hookup, backloop, hookup, backloop...Make three hookups from 7200 ft. this way.	75%
4	3-man, backloop, 3-man, backloop...Twice from 7200 ft.	70%
5	Delay your exit from one to three seconds and still enter, or pin, cleanly from 7200 ft.	80%
6	Be part of a 4-man built in 12 sec. or less	65%

If you are proficient at the above, your RW skill will speak a lot more convincingly than your mouth and you'll find yourself on more and more large-star loads as your skill progresses.

Closed Loads

Sometimes when you are trying to do your thing ... which happens to be RW ... you find that you can't get on the kind of RW loads you want on. It nearly feels as if you're being persecuted.

But there are other reasons why a load may be "closed" to an RW novice. Conversation with serious competition team members may shed some light on the subject. Here are some typical comments from RW competitors:

"People don't realize that jumping with unknowns is scary. ... (Like all of parachuting) RW is risky. To do hot RW you must have FAITH in everyone on the load. An 'unknown' can destroy you and/or the star ... I've seen it happen."

"I spend a lot of time and a lot of money to be good enough to do RW well. When I go out and someone's bombed the star it makes me mad. You don't ever need to bomb a star. When I had RW learning problems I corrected them on small star loads. Everybody should do likewise."

"During the months before a big RW meet every competitor (unfortunately) goes nuts and nasty trying to get his act together for the meet. There's just no time for fun jumps ... my pocketbook can only afford team jumps."

Perhaps you've done a lot of small-star relative work but are new to the big star arena. Or you may be visiting a different drop zone. Naturally you want to make a swoop and get in some good RW. In these cases you'll probably be asked what your qualifications are.

That's perfectly normal and prudent. If you're SCR/SCS, say so. If you've earned one of the 16 or larger patches, or jumped in RW competition, then mention that, too. If you don't have much big-star experience but are a 100%-er in a pin, 3rd or 4th position, tell the starmaster that.

Don't babble. Just state the facts. Let your RW speak for itself. Skill speaks loudest with silence. The starmaster will assign you a slot. Unless you can't handle it, take it and prepare to have fun.

You'll be up there doing something you love to do. You're not paying money to prove something or to "show them." The easiest thing to forget in such a situation is the fact that you jump for the joy of jumping.

The vibes emitted by a positive attitude will help everyone. Mainly though, you'll have a good time ... and even if it turns out to be just watching people fly around a tumbling base, it's something you can't see on television!

On a Big Star Load At Last!

If you happen to be a nervous novice here are some hints that may help you.

Where to Exit. When you first start doing RW from aircraft larger than you're used to, spend at least two jumps going last and not trying to get in. Just get the feel of the aircraft, the exit, tracking, etc. When you are comfortable try to go out 4th or 5th or 6th.

You'll be a bit too nervous to handle base-pin-3rd positions properly, and these are key to the whole jump. Also, these first three slots involve a lot of difficult sub-terminal RW. The star load depends on your getting in when you're supposed to. That's pressure you don't need.

Going seventh or later involves too much diving, tracking and high speed approaches—and not enough close-in RW and star flying. You want to learn large-star RW, not track for 20 seconds.

Going in the middle of the load gives you a lot of time to make a good, leisurely, skillful approach and entry. Additionally it gives you a margin for error so you can re-approach if you miss your first try.

No one expects you to be perfect right from the start. However, everyone does rightfully expect you to act sensibly and to place the integrity of the star above your own desire to "get in," to "be faster" or similar ego trips. If you do a good job and give it a well-controlled try, you'll be asked on more loads even if you don't always get in.

But bomb the star, approach too hot, go below and

loiter there, and you'll build a bad reputation long before you build a star. Exhibit self-control.

Listen! When you do get on a big RW load, listen closely to the starmaster. He will give you a flying assignment which you are expected to carry out. You will be judged on your ability to follow directions, so listen.

Do not talk too much on the ride up. You're probably tense enough and babbling just signals this to others. If you are talking, you can't be listening.

Dig the sky and the clouds. Clear your mind, put your will in control. Except for the number of participants, you are going up to do something you've done before—good relative work. Try to build a positive, relaxed attitude about it.

Making your Exit. Making your first several exits for big-star work can be unsettling. Exits are hard to control. If you let yourself get rattled by a bad exit, the rest of your jump reflects that state of mind. So do yourself a favor and remember that the exit is just part of a whole sequence of things that make up the jump.

Get solidly into the exit lineup. Concentrate on getting into the count and sway of it. First work on just getting out the door. If you hit the door jamb or "Z" out the door, resolve not to panic or overcompensate (overamp) on the rest of the jump.

When you find yourself outside the aircraft in the unfamiliar subterminal air, you'll have a tendency to "fight it" in your efforts to get squared away quickly. You may be confused because the Relative Wind is coming from the direction of the airplane's travel rather than from below as you'd expect. But if you stiffen your mind and body to "regain control," you'll lose the relaxed edge required for the rest of the jump.

Relaxing your entire body is the answer. Your arms, legs and torso will automatically find the direction of the Relative Wind for you just as feathers find it for a dart or an arrow.

Relax, let your mind take control, and you can begin doing the RW that you've worked so long to learn. And by not rushing to "catch up," you'll likely find that your entry time will be respectable anyway.

If you lose sight of the star because you've Z-ed out, don't get frantic. Relax. Go into a shallow dive, find the others on your load who are making a bee-line for the star, and follow them.

Approach. As you're aiming at the star, plan to stop dead still at a spot about 30 feet outside the star and off to one side. Be sure your stopping spot is about 15 to 20 ft. above the level of the star. Stop with a full flare, then begin a final approach to dock.

The reason for stopping is important. As a novice you don't have enough experience to know when you're in "full stop" in relation to the star. You'll tend to see movement as coming from the star and not from yourself. You have to *stop* to be sure—at least for your first few attempts. Otherwise you'll end up sliding around the star and you could bomb it...or someone near it.

You aim to the side of the star for the same reason. If you aim directly at the star and misjudge your stopping point by 10 feet, you'll likely sail right through the star. Maybe you won't hit anyone. Maybe you will.

If you stop 15 to 20 feet above the star, you'll retain some altitude to convert back into forward momentum to make a forceful and precise final approach without undue effect from the "burble," or wall of turbulent air around the star.

If you find yourself stuck in a slot and unable to lay your hands on wrists, going stiff and reaching for them won't help. You must flare up and back out of the slot so you can swoop in again with enough momentum to carry you onto wrists. You'll need to back at least eight feet out and six feet up to attempt a re-approach. Use a recovery position to accomplish this.

Docking and Entry. As a novice, touching wrists will at first send such a charge of adrenalin through you that you'll probably stiffen, float, and mess up.

When you dock on wrists or wherever, do not do anything else until you relax and settle to fly *with* the star.

A premature entry can endanger the star. A slow entry affects nothing except the traffic of others waiting to get in behind you. Since you're a novice, entering slowly and carefully is not only acceptable, it is preferred.

When you have a good, solid grip on a wrist or a jumpsuit, and are flying with the star, shake and break to enter. Now relax and dig it. (But don't forget that you still have to help fly the star.)

Break-off and Pull. At breakoff time ALWAYS do a 180° turn and track away from the star until opening time. To pull early, to fail to track away, or to track for the spot can easily get you killed or hurt. A large percentage of RW-related fatalities occur because of failure to get properly clear of the contact area.

At pull time ALWAYS give a wave-off and check around and above you before pulling. Do not sit up to pull, because you will backslide toward the contact area and a possible collision.

Do not pull above 3500 ft. Pulling higher on an RW load is dangerous and marks you as a nitwit. Pulling higher means everyone has to stop doing RW and worry about an open canopy in the area.

If someone in your area dumps while you're still in freefall, dive away from him immediately. If you've missed his body and canopy, wait until he gets line stretch before you pull. If you pull before he gets full line stretch, you could end up eating canopy. Remember that most canopies surge forward at peak opening pressure.

Once you have inflation, check around you for other open canopies. Have your hands on the toggles. Be ready to make a quick turn to avoid an entanglement.

Doing all of this is not hard if you've preconditioned yourself on other jumps and on the ground. Of course, the easiest thing to do in a tight situation is nothing. But remember, the easiest thing of all is to get killed. The important thing about proper break-off and pull procedures for RW is that you *do* them.

After the Jump. Don't expect everyone to feel the same way about the jump as you do. Some will be happy with their performance; others will be down because they feel they flew like turkeys.   Only about a third of the jumpers will have actually seen what went on, and most of those will disagree on some points.

After an RW jump it's a good idea to listen to what other people on the load have to say. If you feel compelled to talk, remember that whatever you say is probably heavily influenced by the exciting things that went on, and that the resulting adrenalin rush reduces your ability to communicate courteously or completely.

To be more to the point: If you don't have anything positive to say, then *say nothing.* If you cannot come across with good vibes, then keep the negative things to yourself. Don't spit in the soup that you'll have to eat later.

If you really feel you have to bumrap the jump, it's a good idea to go pack your rig first. Then perhaps you can be more objective about it. Bad vibes is a sickness that can destroy teams, dropzones, friendships and fun. Is it worth it?

If you made a serious mistake on the jump you'll know it, of course, and you'll hear about it. But if you did okay, or didn't do as well as you'd wished and don't know why, then wait a bit, try to remember accurately everything that happened, and talk it over with one of the more experienced RW'ers who was on the load.

Jumping With a Team

As you gain more experience, you may decide to jump with a team, whether it be for serious competition or just for the security of always having a group of people to jump with.

Jumping with a team can be a very rewarding experience. You can learn much about RW by jumping with the same people most of the time—they'll be a constant against which you can practice your flying techniques. You'll be able to see more clearly, jump after jump, what your body is actually doing in relation to the others.

Every team jump is planned in advance. You'll take

your assigned place in the lineup on jump run, and your exit will be better because of your familiarity with the count and sway of the team.

Outside the plane, you'll always know where the star is and what your flight pattern should be. You'll be familiar with the falling speed of the star so that your flare point is not a matter of guesswork.

In the star, you'll feel the charge of good vibes that flows around the circle when you all know it's a good jump. The electricity of a team, trying its best to work together to build a fast star or an intricate formation, is very exciting.

Note: Portions of this chapter were specially rewritten for *Regnery Guide to Sport Parachuting*, published by Henry Regnery Company, Chicago. Copyright© 1974 by Charles W. Ryan.

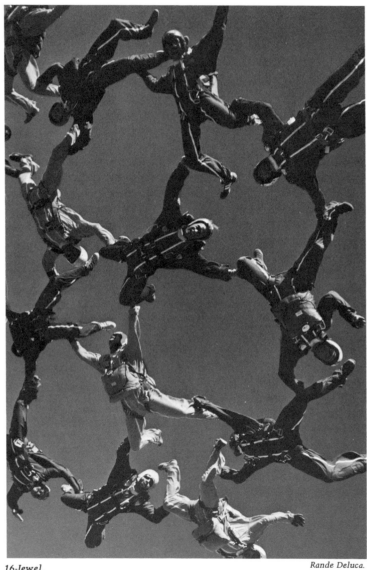

16-Jewel.   *Rande Deluca.*

Chapter XV
For the RW Expert

 Freefall Relative Work is where it is today now. Later never exists and yesterday won't come again. RW just happened and grew. Being non-created, it is transcendent over acceptance or rejection. Unfettered, it does not ossify into ritual mechanistics and so continues to grow. Since it is represented and led by *participants* rather than a ground-hog "leader," it grows. If directed by a brotherhood of freefallers, this growth can strengthen us through unity in numbers. We are all just beginning. Let's begin together. Do some RW on the ground so we can do lots of it in the air.

Fundamental Courtesies of Relative Work

1. RW loads involve others beside yourself—be considerate of their time and their feelings.

2. It is impolite to be consistently late rigging up for a load so as to make others wait for you.

3. Enter the airplane in reverse exit order. Trying to reshuffle people in the proper exit lineup on jumprun is an unnecessary distraction.

4. The pilot is in command of the aircraft until jumprun and the "cut." He may need your help collecting tickets, shifting forward for take-off, etc. Help make his job easier.

5. ALWAYS give the countdown and exit your best effort. You may be good enough to loaf out the door, but it's not fair to impede those behind you. If you don't like fast exits, go last or as a floater where you are out of the way.

6. The integrity of the star is more important than your desire to get in fast. Don't bomb it. Get a *good* grip before entering.

7. If you go low, do not loiter beneath the approach area.

8. Always go for the assigned base man. If the pin man or someone else goes low, the star should not try to fly down to help him out.

9. Fly smoothly so as not to impede those behind you. Do not orbit the star in the approach area.

10. ALWAYS do a 180° turn and track away at break-off altitude. Look around you before you pull.

11. If you go low or can't get in, DO NOT pull high while the others are still linked in a star.

12. When you land, make it a rule never to bad-rap the jump you've just made. Others had fun, even if you didn't. Why spoil it for them?

13. There's a lot of adrenalin still in your system when you land. Use that energy to pack up for the next jump rather than to berate your fellow jumpers.

14. Remember, when someone makes a mistake they feel a lot worse about it than you do. Be gentle with the other person's ego.

15. Try to suppress *your* ego when you become a Skygod. Helping others to be as good as you are pays richer dividends than does creating tension. Remember that your SCR or SCS number, how many jumps you have, and/or how long you've been jumping don't really relate to doing relative work on your next jump.

16. Yesterday never returns; later never exists—do RW now!

The Etiquette of Large-Star Building

About 80 to 85 per cent of the large-star (16-man and larger) attempts made fall apart, or are taken out, by 6,000 ft. or higher. I can recall only a couple of large stars in which I've participated that were flown down to break-off altitude. Far too many shatter into so many one-man stars while there is still a good 20-30 seconds of working time left.

Since there are really only three major causes of small stars when you're trying for a BIG one, you would think people would learn, and after a suitable period of time, quit making the same mistakes over and over. They learn, but once they exit on the next attempt, they forget.

Here are the three biggest reasons for unsuccessful 16-man or larger star attempts:

1. Going too fast (over-amping, the ego—ME! I got in!!)
2. Going rigid in the star (becoming overly stiff, not flying the star properly.)
3. Lost grip.

These are such simple problems, so widely known, that enough people will downgrade the importance of these reasons on *your* big-star attempt so that you'll be tracking away by 6,000 ft., too.

Why do people get so gobbled up with ego or tension? Why do the people who build that all important 10-man base tense up? It shouldn't happen because it's something they've done perfectly countless times before. Why do the guys in the back of the load feel they must go so fast? They can do RW well or they wouldn't have been invited on the load. Failure to concentrate on their assigned job is the probable reason.

On a serious attempt for a 16-man or larger, the manifestors of the load know you can do RW well before your name goes on the list. The exit order is determined mainly by the 10-man base. You want the best, most solid 10-man base you can have. Often competition 10-man star teams base for large-star attempts. They can build a fast, sturdy, well-flown 10-man base formation under pressure; one which other select RW'ers can enter. Positions in the rest of the exit order are then assigned by someone who has an idea about the capabilities of those on the load.

After the manifesting, a meeting is usually called for all participants by the manifestor or starmaster. This meeting may take many forms, however, there are several key topics to be covered:

1. *The exit order.* Everyone should line up so they'll know who they follow.
2. *The countdown for exit.* This should be practiced by the first ten.

3. *Spotting and relay of signals to pilot.* Touch on this only briefly with the jumpers, but have a separate briefing for the pilot(s). This is particularly important if several aircraft are involved.
4. *Assigned entry quadrants of the star.*
5. *The Five Commandments of Large-Star Building.*
   a. Thou Shalt Exit Fast.
   b. Thou Shalt Fly SLOW.
   c. Thou Shalt Enter Cleanly.
   d. Thou Shalt Get a Good Grip.
   e. Thou Shalt Turn and TRACK at Breakoff.

It is very hard to get large groups of people together, particularly relative workers. Nevertheless, organization on large stars pays off, as evidenced by the tremendous amount of planning that resulted in California's 31-man star.

Organizers need just the right touch of authority and expertise. The first ten in the 31-man record were members of a competition 10-man team. Every individual on the load was capable of flying any position in the exit lineup. Each member of the 10-man base had the back of their helmets marked with a criss-cross of red tape. The second ten, marked similarly with yellow tape, were to enter between two reds.

The ever-present traffic problem was solved by giving everyone a consecutive number in the exit order. Even numbers were to approach from the right side; odd numbers from the left side.

To ensure good grips, each jumper had sewn an 8 to 10-inch length of flexible ⅝ths inch rubber hose inside the lower part of each arm bell of his jumpsuit.

Grips are especially important on a large-star attempt where a considerable amount of pressure may be put on the grips in a small area of the star. Because lost grips are a major cause of large-star failure, extra attention should be given to getting a firm grip before breaking into the star.

When making repeated jumps from 13,000 ft. above sea level or higher, it is important to recognize at the outset that most everyone will suffer from hypoxia. Participants should not move around unnecessarily. If you want to experience hypoxia, just try to whistle row-row-row-your-boat twice while at altitude. Hypoxia slows your thinking and reflexes, not the best conditions for building big stars.

There are two ways to measure the size of stars. The F.A.I. requires prior notification, and then observation of a star held a minimum of five seconds by an F.A.I. judge, for an "official" world record. The American rule is stated simply: "If it's not on film, then it's not a valid record size star."

The Tradition of Relative Work: Teaching It

Active relative workers are encouraged to improve and maintain the good vibes of RW. Your goal should be to promote parachuting in general, and relative work in particular. RW is a beautiful, exhilarating experience which you'll want to help others enjoy.

It took those of us who've been into RW for awhile a long time to learn it because there was no one to teach us. Because it was difficult for us to master, we sometimes forget that now we have the skills to teach this art to novices.

They'll learn much faster than we did because they won't make our mistakes. One of the quickest ways to build bigger stars is to have more qualified jumpers to build them.

In order to do relative work, you have to relate to others in the air. This has created a brotherhood of free-fallers. As brothers and sisters we should help each other, from the national and international level, all the way down to your group at the local DZ.

It's our sport. We must try to avoid ego trips, politics and hassles. We should promote those aspects of the sport which foster the brotherhood.

Every accomplished RW'er should work with novices to impart not only the mechanical skills required to fly the body, but also the attitude that releases the ecstasy of freefall relative work.

To do good relative work, you must have a fairly large group of proficient people to relate in freefall with. The better the overall RW level of your group, the better the RW you'll be able to participate in. This requires RW "skull" sessions and active training programs for RW novices.

As in any sport, there is a constant loss of participants who get married, move away, burn out, etc. Who will replace them? If it took you 300 jumps to learn RW, don't you now know enough to teach a novice in a lot less time? Want too build a 16-man star or a 16-man snowflake or some other presently out-of-reach goal at your DZ? Shouldn't you invest a little of your time in training others to do RW?

There is a natural Brotherhood of Relative Workers. We all work together to perform aerial artistry. Throughout history other groups have recognized their inherent brotherhood. They formalized it enough to keep the group strong, healthy, happy and growing. They laid down tenets of friendship, service, courtesy, hospitality, and training. The Masons, Elks, Shriners and others are good examples.

When you work with a novice, you're not just teaching the mechanics of flying—you're imparting a good, positive feeling toward your sport. You are hospitable and friendly to visitors and novices, not because you are basically a nice guy, but because you realize that only a big group of brothers in the sky can perform intricate large-star freefall relative work maneuvers successfully.

A very real problem, of course, is the novice with a big ego who won't see and won't listen. This case doesn't take instruction very well, and usually refuses to learn even the basic maneuvers. They're like the people who go to a movie and never see the picture.

My advice is to leave them to their own devices. Concentrate on someone who *wants* to learn. *Just five jumps with an interested novice will give him experience and knowledge of techniques that took you 50 jumps to learn.*

Do this in the spring, and you'll have your big dream star by fall. And, brother, you'll have a lot of fun getting there.

Working With the Novice Relative Worker

Here is a study plan you may use to teach relative work:

First, give the student a friendly, brief introduction to the art of freefall relative work. Anyone making controlled 30-second delays is a good candidate. Emphasize the beauty and things *you* like about RW. Tell him of the brotherhood he's about to join.

7500 Feet, Phase I. Prerequisites are enthusiasm for RW and ability to perform these basic freefall maneuvers:

1. Turns
2. Track
3. Clear (waveoff) to pull
4. Unpoised, bomb-out-the-door exits
5. Aircraft exit from the reserve "pin" position (facing the tail, his back to the strut of a Cessna-182)

7500 Feet, First RW Jump. The student's assignment is to concentrate on making a stable exit. He picks a heading and holds it. He thinks about relaxing; his seeing or not seeing the pin man (you) isn't as important as his relaxing and enjoying the jump. In fact, seeing the instructor should key and reinforce the student's will to relax his mind and body in order to fully enjoy his first closing, docking, and entry. The instructor concentrates on perfectly controlled, clean airwork. Do not pin the student until after terminal is reached. Make a nice, slow, clean entry if your novice is relaxed enough to allow it.

7500 Feet, Second RW Jump. The student's preliminary assignment is the same as above. After this hookup, the instructor tucks up and allows the student to level out the two-man. Time permitting, the instructor next spreads out and again allows the student to level it out. The purpose of this jump is to get the novice RW'er accustomed to the idea and mechanics of flying in contact with others. Smile.

7500 Feet, Third Jump. It starts just as do the first two. After the hookup the instructor raises one leg, turning the star. The student's assignment is to stop the turn and then reverse its direction.

7500 Feet, Fourth Jump. Again, hook up after terminal velocity has been reached. After the initial hookup, the instructor backs off ten feet and lets the student try to close for a possible second two-man. Discuss floating, vertical rate of descent, reverse arch, and the necessity to pull before impact.

7500 Feet, Phase II. Graduation from student to novice! Student exits second from the pin slot. The student does as much of the relative work as possible. If successful, repeat the fourth-jump maneuvers.

Here are some other suggestions for teaching relative work:

Ground practice is especially important to a novice so he will know before the jump what will happen and how to do his part. Cover the basics of doing RW one thing at a time. For example, the exit is important but a bad exit doesn't mess up an entire jump unless the novice lets it by over-reacting to it. It is but a single mistake that is only a part of the jump. Just call it the Great Chain of Creation, with interdependent links.

After the jump, ask the novice what he thought went on during the jump before you give your critique. This makes him think about it and gives you an idea how alert he is.

When criticizing RW performance on a jump, be SURE to mention those things done correctly. He even may not have been aware of what he was doing right. Most people respond well to praise and positive reinforcement, and since a lot of jumps are relived throughout the following week, it provides some positive thoughts to dwell on.

Novices like having three or four things planned for a jump: say a three-man, backloop, three-man; or break it into a line and fly it back together again. If the first three-man is fast you can use the rest of the jump for more learning, and if it is slow you still had a three-man!

No jump with a novice relative worker is a waste of either time or money, especially if he or she really wants the help. You have the ability to reveal one of life's great experiences—a very natural high—and you'll both dig it.

★   ★   ★

Relative work is "new"—we've hardly begun. If we start today to plant the seed for a growing tradition of friendship, we'll be able to reap the many pleasures of relating to others in the air for a long time to come.

Every one of us is a one-man star. To build something bigger we must do relative work.

ABOUT THE AUTHOR

Pat and Jan Works

Pat is an active participant in all phases of freefall relative work, including innovative fun-jumping, serious competitive jumping, and teaching relative work to others.

As a competitor, he jumped most recently with 10-man and 4-man teams at the 1978 National Parachuting Championships, serving as captain of both teams, called "First Formation." Other relative work teams with which he has competed as a member include the Chaos 8-man sequential teams (1976-77), Element of Chance (1976), the Western Conference Four-Man Team (1974), the James Gang (1972-73), Godfrogs (1972) and Avis (1971).

Pat was a member of a three-man committee which successfully proposed the 10-man relative work event for the U.S.P.A. National Championships in 1972. He competed in that first 10-Man Nationals and also in the national 4-man event that year.

He has also competed in style and accuracy, with the Texas A&M University team (1962-64), Wallace's Outlaws (1964-65), and the University of Houston Parachute Team (1965-67).

As a relative work trainer, Pat has conducted several relative work camps, including one in Maubeuge (France) and another in Meissendorf (West Germany). Pat uses a combination of classroom lectures, demonstrations and practice jumps under his direction to teach novice jumpers how to master relative work techniques quickly, safely, and with an attitude of joy in flying.

Pat started jumping in Texas in 1961. He helped organize and was editor for the Texas Parachute Council. He was founder and president of the University of Houston Parachute Club, which won the team event at the 1966 National Collegiate Parachuting Championships.

Pat's wife Jan is also an active relative worker, with more than 1,000 jumps accumulated since her first in 1970. She, too, has jumped competitively with several 10-man and 4-man teams, including Madame Sally's Sky Hookers (1976-77) and the Godfrogs (1973). She was one of the organizers of the first all-women's 8-way star on the East Coast (1973), and has participated in several other women's records attempts, including the first all-women's (11) night star (1977).

Pat and Jan published the *RWunderground* newsletter from 1972-76 to serve as the first communications medium for promoting the growth of relative work parachuting. They also established the annual C.G. Godfrog Good-Vibes Award, the RW Council's Certificates of Merit, and the annual National Champion of Combined RW Awards.

Pat has had articles and stories published in every major parachuting publication, and has received special awards of appreciation from the French National RW Team (1973) and the Australian Parachute Federation for his efforts in promoting relative work competition worldwide. *The Art of Freefall Relative Work* has been adopted as the standard reference text of freefall flying in a number of countries.

Pat and Jan recently released their second book, *United We Fall*, a relative work anthology of stories and articles written by relative workers for relative workers, and including "the best of *RWunderground*."

SCS-1
SCR-561
1800 jumps
USPA Class D "Expert" license, Jumpmaster

GLOSSARY

Accuracy—An event in the individual competition. Each jumper attempts to land as close as possible to a 10cm target on the ground. This is considered one of two classic events.

Boogie—The term was brought back from the New Zealand International Parachuting Competition. It applies to having a great time either jumping, dancing, partying, or going away to a parachuting meet, etc.

Braking—Manipulating the steering controls and vent so as to slow or halt the forward inherent canopy speed without changing direction.

Breakoff Point—The altitude established prior to a jump whereby all jumpers stop relative work and spread out in preparation to safely open their parachutes away from one another.

Canopy Speed (Forward Speed)—The inherent horizontal speed of a canopy generated by the control of cloth porosity and the deflection of escaping air through specifically designed control or escape vents.

Dead Center—A perfect score on an accuracy jump. Each competitor attempts to touch a 10cm target as the first point of contact.

Deployment Bag—The safety device encasing the parachute canopy which (1) creates drag thereby decreasing opening chock and (2) insures that the suspension lines are fully extended prior to canopy inflation, thereby preventing jumper entanglement with the deploying canopy.

Dirt Diving—Ground practice, usually just prior to boarding the airplane. The jumpers walk through their intended maneuvers in the sequences of the actual jump. Helps develop rhythm and awareness of each persons task, as well as motivating each to do their best.

Docking—In sequential relative work, two or more formations separate and rejoin to complete a new or different formation.

Drop Zone—The open area or field surrounding the central target area designated for the landing of parachutists.

Eight Man—An event in the relative work competition. Eight jumpers have a specified amount of time to perform required formations.

Equipment Check—The final visual and physical check of the equipment made by the jumpmaster on all parachutists prior to boarding the aircraft.

Exit Point—A predetermined point on the ground over which the jumpers leave the aircraft to land in a specified area.

Experienced Parachutist—Person with over 200 parachute freefall jumps.

Four Man—An event in the relative work competition. Four jumpers have a specified amount of time to perform required formations.

Freefall—Jumping without an attachment between the parachute and the aircraft and delaying (over three seconds) the opening of the parachute. The higher the jump the longer the delay.

Funnel—In relative work, a formation collapses or breaks up by sinking from the middle. Usually caused by improper flying and too great a concentration of jumpers in one area.

Intermediate Parachutist—Person with more than 50 but less than 200 parachute freefall jumps.

Jump and Pull—Jumping and clearing the aircraft and immediately pulling the ripcord (within three seconds).

Jump Run—The final leg of flight just prior to exiting the aircraft. Varies in length based on the number exiting, type and style of aircraft, altitude, etc.

Leading Zone—The place on the airfield where the jumping list or manifest is made up and jumpers wait their turn to board the aircraft.

Log Book—The individual jump record book in which a jumper keeps a chronological record of each jump similar to a pilot's log book. Used for verifying jumping experience for licensing, competition, etc.

Malfunction—Any improper functioning of the parachute system.

Novice Parachutist—Person with less than 50 freefall parachute jumps.

Opening Altitude—2,500 feet above the ground.

Opening Shock—The tug or jerk felt by the jumper as the canopy opens and fully inflates. The degree of intensity is influenced by factors such as vertical and horizontal velocity, atmospheric condition, body position, type of parachute, method of deployment, etc. However, the standard sport parachutes in common use today contribute surprisingly little or no discomfort when properly activated.

Parachute Club—A local, autonomous, and non-commercial grouping of parachutists whos primary purpose is to enjoy the fun of parachuting. Most clubs conduct training for their own new students and may or may not be affiliated with U.S. Parachute Association.

Para Commander—An older, but highly reliable oval-shaped competition canopy of French design.

Pig Rig—Equipment worn by most relative workers. Both main and reserve parachutes are worn on the back. Also called a tandem or piggy back system.

Pilot Chute—A small spring loaded parachute which springs or leaps out into the jumpers slipstream when released by the ripcord pull. Attached to a deployment bag, it acts as dragging anchor to lift and deploy the parachute assembly until the main parachute canopy inflates.

PLF's (Parachute Landing Falls)—The method of falling down on landing by which the jumper resists, absorbs, and distributes the landing impact over various parts of the body rather than on just the feet, ankles and legs.

Pull Out Pilot Chute—A deployment device used to start the opening sequence of the main parachute. It has no spring and is usually folded in a small pouch on the jumpers waist. The pilot chute is pulled out of the pouch and held in the wind stream to inflate. Also called a throw out pilot chute.

Ram Air Parachutes—The newest designs in canopies. Rectangular in shape, it performs similar to an aircraft wing and offers a high glide ratio and speed and is very accurate for competition.

Relative Work—The cooperative aerial maneuvers executed by two or more jumpers during freefall in order to pass batons, create or "hook up" various formations, or for air-to-air photography. Such group maneuvering is tricky, due to many variables, and success is normally attained only by the more experienced parachutists.

Ripcord—The metal handle and attached steel cable and locking pins which hold the parachute closed until the jumper pulls it loose, thereby unlocking the pack and freeing the pilot chute and canopy to deploy.

Sequential R/W—A popular form of skydiving where groups of jumpers build different formations in the sky in a particular sequence. Oftentimes these formations are separate and flown back together again.

Skygod—A term to describe relative work jumpers who talk better than they jump. Usually a close cousin of a whuffo.

Sport Parachuting (Sky Diving or Jumping)—The art of exiting from an aircraft over the proper point at a high altitude, stabilizing the body during a free or delayed fall, executing various controlled body maneuvers—either alone or with others—safely opening the parachute at a given time and point, and then controlling the parachute so as to land safely on a specific ground target.

Spotting—The technique of selecting the course to fly, directing the pilot, dropping the wind drift indicator, selecting the correct ground reference point over which to (1) exit from the aircraft and (2) open the parachute.

Star—A term which is applied to a hook-up of 5 or more jumpers holding each others' wrists. The formation which is achieved resembles a star from the ground.

Steering Lines (Toggles, Knobs)—The special lines and their handles which are attached to key control panels and vents to "drive" the parachute canopy by controlling the angle and shape of the vents which affect the horizontal and vertical canopy speed and the direction.

Style—An event in the individual competition. Each jumper has 25 seconds to do a series of 360° turns and loops. The competitors are judged on time and headings. This is considered one of two classic events.

Ten Man—Often referred to as the 100 yd. dash of relative work. Ten skydivers exit an airplane and form a round circle in the fastest time.

Terminal Velocity—The greatest speed at which a body falls through the atmosphere (176 feet per second or 120 m.p.h.), which is constant after the 12th second of freefall.

Trac—A competitive event combining accuracy and relative work. A team of four jumpers perform various maneuvers in freefall and land on a predetermined target. The team is judged on time and total distance.

United States Parachute Association (USPA)—The only national sport parachuting organization in the United States dedicated solely to the promotion, improvement, and safety of parachuting and the parachutist. It also selects and trains the United States Parachute Team and enters it into international and world championship competition.

Whuffo—The term now generally applied to non-jumping spectators. The term originated earlier in agricultural areas when curious farmers paused in their work to inquire, "Whuffo you-all jump outta them pair-chutes?"

Wind Line—An imaginary wind direction line extending from the true opening point to the target center. Such lines vary in direction and velocity at different altitudes. The accuracy competitor attempts to stay on this wind line until he touches the target.

Wind Streamer—A narrow length of colored and weighted paper or cloth dropped prior to the start of jumping to measure wind speed and direction to assist in selecting the proper exit and opening point. The indicator has approximately the same rate of descent as a parachutist with an open canopy.

ZAP—Zero All Points. Occurs when a competitor or team makes enough mistakes which causes a loss of all points.

Mike Horan

Team Chaos.   *M. Anderson Jenkins.*

Team Chaos.   *M. Anderson Jenkins.*

MANEUVERS
SECTION

INTRODUCTION

All maneuvers and sequential relative work start with a hook-up. This hook-up is the key to the rest of the maneuver. There are five basic hook-ups:

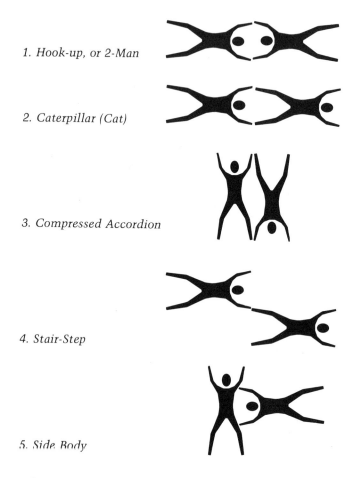

1. Hook-up, or 2-Man

2. Caterpillar (Cat)

3. Compressed Accordion

4. Stair-Step

5. Side Body

The possible combinations which can be built from these fundamental hook-ups are limited only by your skill and imagination.

Fig. 1.
THE BI-POLE (2 Methods)

Method 1:

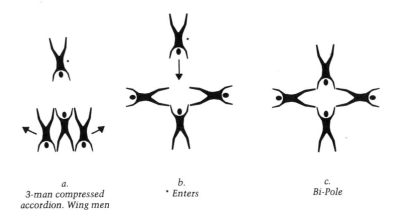

a.
3-man compressed accordion. Wing men fold-out to present legs to *.

b.
* Enters

c.
Bi-Pole

Method 2:

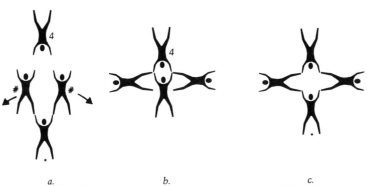

a.
* Enters on legs of a 2-man line to form base. At *'s signal, # fold-out to present legs to 4.

b.
4 Enters

c.
* Backs out to form bi-pole

Fig. 2.

DONUT (How to Build a Donut)+

a.	*b.*	*c.*
Base. Simultaneously, each flyer puts his left hand on his own left knee. This allows each flyer to grab the proffered knee with his right hand.	Flyers put hand to knee—grip change. Look into the center-switch on signal.	Change grips to get right hand outboard. Hold hand above head to stop spinning; look into the center—fly.

Fig. 3.

DONUT DOUBLE FLAKE

a.
Maneuver built from a
donut base.

+For alternate method of building a donut, see Fig. #5(a-c).

Fig. 4.
BI-POLE TO A DONUT

a.
Bi-pole base, drop grips at
o; * fold out to form (b).

b.
Double compressed
accordion. * grab leg.

c.
Drop grip o; # grip
change.

d.
Donut

(0 = break grip)

Fig. 5.

MULTIPLE 4-MAN MANEUVERS (ONE JUMP)

a.
Compressed accordion base.

b.
Opposed diamond

c.
* *Grip-switch to donut.*

d.
Drop grip and fold-out to (e).

e.
Caterpillar

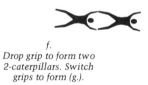

f.
Drop grip to form two 2-caterpillars. Switch grips to form (g.).

g.
Left hand stair-steps.

h.
Left hand stair-steps. Dock into facing diamond.

Fig. 6.
SEQUENTIAL 5-DOUBLE DONUT

a.
Compressed accordion
base.

b.

c.
5-Double Donut.

Fig. 7.
4-MAN MANEUVER SET

a.
Bi-pole.

c.
Compressed accordion.

b.
Folds in to form (c).

d.
Drops grips and folds-out
to form (e).

e.
Caterpillar (tracks)

Fig. 8.
BI-FLAKED BI-POLE

Fig. 9.
TRIPOD

Fig. 10.
9-CLUSTER

Fig. 11.
12-CLUSTER

Fig. 12.
TRI-DIAMONDS

Fig. 13.
EAGLE TO FRENCH CONNECTION

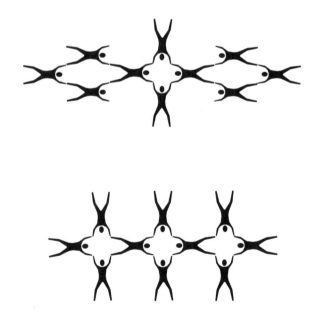

Fig. 14.
EAGLE (Variation)

Fig. 15.
THE WEDGE

Fig. 16.
HOUR GLASS

Fig. 17.
9-DIAMOND

* *Good pull-out*

Fig. 18.
TRIPLE DIAMONDS

Fig. 19.
TRIPLE HORIZONTAL DIAMONDS

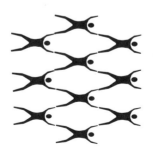

Fig. 20.

SEQUENCE DOUBLE DIAMOND TO FOUR POINT SNOWFLAKE

a.
Double Diamond to:

b.
4-Point Snowflake.

Fig. 21.

JAMES GANG
SPEED STAR MANEUVER "A"
(Involves a Lot of Flying)

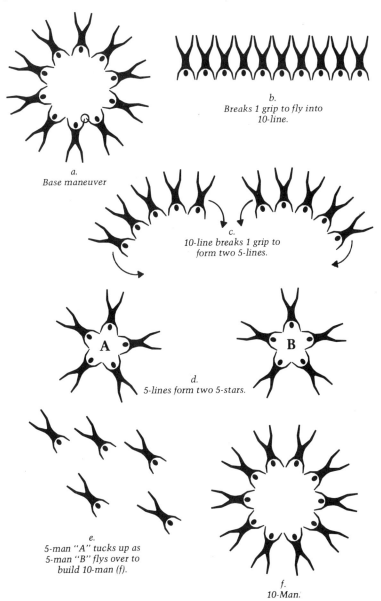

b.
Breaks 1 grip to fly into
10-line.

a.
Base maneuver

c.
10-line breaks 1 grip to
form two 5-lines.

d.
5-lines form two 5-stars.

e.
5-man "A" tucks up as
5-man "B" flys over to
build 10-man (f).

f.
10-Man.

Fig. 22.

ALL STARS SPEED STAR MANEUVER "B"

a.
Base maneuver

b.
Breaks into two 5-man
lines which close (c).

c.
"S"-line closes ends in.

d.
Closed double lines.

(0 = break grip)

e.
Drop grip to form second
10-man star.

Fig. 23.

DARE TO BE GREAT
(A 10-Man Sequence Involving a Lot of Flying)

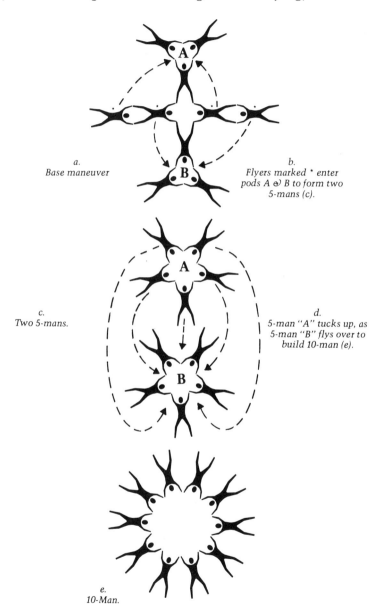

a.
Base maneuver

b.
*Flyers marked * enter
pods A & B to form two
5-mans (c).*

c.
Two 5-mans.

d.
*5-man "A" tucks up, as
5-man "B" flies over to
build 10-man (e).*

e.
10-Man.

Fig. 24.

DOUBLE DIAMOND DOCK TO FORM
AN EAGLE

Fig. 25.
THE 8-MAN IN-OUT (How to Do It)

a.
Bi-pod.

b.
Pods fold back to form....

c.
Double compressed
accordion.

d.
Leg men enter....

e.
Base-2 drop grips....

f.
The 8-man in-out.

Fig. 26.

SEQUENTIAL MANEUVER:
TRIPLE DIAMOND TO DIAMOND DOCK TO FORM
AN EAGLE

a.
Triple diamond

b.
Sequence

c.
Diamond Dock

d.
Eagle

Fig. 27.
16-MAN DIAMOND

Fig. 28.
16-MAN QUADRAPOD

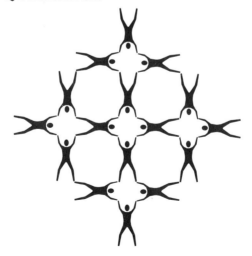

Fig. 29.
16-MAN QUADRA-DIAMOND

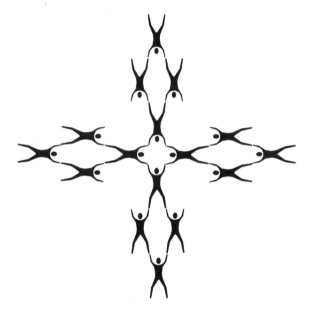

Fig. 30.
20-MAN SNOWFLAKE

MAKING THE DIVE
Collected Helpful Hints

Pick maneuvers that match the ability of those on the load.

Encourage no-contact as a fast way to learn awareness and perfect flight.

Determine positions. Use some of the more experienced people who can build a fast, solid base up front. Use less experienced flyers on the outside edges.

Design an exit which is as fast and efficient as possible. Plan to use floaters.

Gear up and walk through the dive on the ground from exit to break-off at least two or three times. Make sure everyone knows what to do.

Practice exit before takeoff.

Exit as fast and close together as possible.

Build large maneuvers in waves or stages, i.e. in a donut-flake, the flakers should set up and wait until the base is *complete and stable.* Don't enter your slot until your counterpart on the other side of the formation can enter theirs. Never add float or sink to the formation.

Perfect speed is being at the right place at the right time. Perfect speed is being *there* so as to mesh with the flow of the developing dive smoothly.

Always take leg grips at the knee or thigh; never interfere with another's key control surfaces.

All docking should be done so that no momentum is transmitted into the formation.

Some formations float. Anticipate this. Don't go low.

Concentrate on your flying assignment with happy abandon. If everyone does, it will go.

Although our medium is air—don't forget the ground. Those in the base formation must cross-reference the ground to keep the formation from turning or sliding.

When flying formations, all members must fly smoothly and united. For example, in a diamond fly as smoothly as you would fly on your own. Don't over-fly your part. The point man on a diamond initiates turns by bending at the waist toward the direction desired. Braking is primarily the job of the tail person Anticipate the necessary corrections—be smooth and deliberate.

Don't try to salvage a bad approach by hanging on and swinging or climbing your man's legs, etc. Let go and fly back into the formation.

As soon as practical after landing, regroup and walk through the jump as it happened. Analyze and correct mistakes. Emphasize the maneuvers that went well. Use tact.

Think together, fly together, and your whole scene will flow together.

MAIL ORDER
Enjoy these freefall goodies.....

1. "The Art of Freefall Relative Work," called the Bible of RW, considered the standard reference text, newly revised. Explains the technique of perfect flight utilizing the attitude of joy. (ISBN 0-930438-01-9) $7.95

2. "United We Fall," a collection of articles and short stories about skydiving. Includes fiction, jump stories and factual how-to's on every aspect of relative work. Exciting original illustrations. (ISBN 0-930438-02-7) $11.95

3. Skydiving Art Prints...prints of the original illustrations from the book "United We Fall." Lithographed on high quality paper, suitable for framing, limited edition of 10 drawings, black and dark brown duotone. Suite of 10: $20.00

4. "Art of Freefall" poster, silver-foil reproduction, suitable for framing. $5.00

Available from book stores, parachute equipment dealers, or by mail.

- -

How To Order:	quantity	amt. $
1. "The Art of Freefall Relative Work"		
2. "United We Fall"		
3. Skydiving art prints (suite of 10)		
4. Silver-foil "Art of Freefall" poster		
Additional for packing & shipping ($.80 per order)		
Sales tax, if any		
TOTAL ENCLOSED		$

Normal delivery time is 2-4 weeks. California residents, please add 6% sales tax. Overseas orders, please add $4 per book or set of prints for airmail shipping.

Name _____

Address _____

State _____ Zip _____

Country _____

Send your name, address, zip code along with your check or money order (be sure to mention items desired!) to:
RW Underground Publications
1656 Beechwood Avenue
Fullerton, Calif. 92635

GIFTS! Send gifts to your friends. Select items above, and mention with your order:

"Gift from _____ to _____
             (your name)   (name of recipient)

_____ .
                    (address of recipient)

We'll include a handwritten note with the gift.

Exitus Line-up.

The Exit-1. *Kevin Shea.*

The Exit-2.   *Kevin Shea.*

TESTIMONIALS

"You've finally put into words the concepts, ideals and beliefs we've all so long felt. You have grasped the essence of the warm friendship of a golden sunset load, spiced it with the taste of competition, then served it on the plate of learning so that we can all digest it and create our own sky pictures. Thank you so very much for all you have given us."

Billy Bishop, SCR 549, Elsinore, California

"Throughout the book the message comes across—you respect and love people. That aspect alone makes it worth reading...not only for the novice but also the experienced jumpers. I have read it twice and plan to use it for future reference. (I have made over 1100 jumps, and have trained and developed RW jumpers for the past three years.)"

Paul E. Reed, Woodbine, Maryland

"Your Super Book came at just the right time!...I plan to practically memorize it...it answers ALL my questions! You should have called it, 'Everything You Always Wanted to Know About RW But...etc.'"

Judy Simpson, D-334, Boston, Massachusetts

"Please send me another copy of your book. It's really been a help. I'm understanding what I've been doing now and I can explain it to other people. I wish it had come out sooner. We are *all* learning; you have given us a basis for understanding what we learn."

Tony Phelps, SCR 4492

"I consider The Art of Freefall RW the Bible of RW and it is certainly required reading for all relative workers from very beginners to advanced sky Gods. Thank you for your contribution to the sport."

Bobby E. Brown, Texas, SCR 3456, SCS 1755, WSCR 429

"*Required Reading.* The student (of RW) must read "The Art of Freefall Relative Work" by Pat Works. Each relative work instructor should equip himself with a copy of this excellent primer...It's worth its weight in gold!...excellent illustrations, explanations, and definitions."

Jamie Woodward, USPA Conference Director

"Enjoyed your book greatly. Being an RW rookie, it has answered a lot of questions concerning technique. More importantly, it has set an example of the attitude participants should have."

Craig Stevens, South Carolina

"This is an important step in the development of RW." "If heeded will save the reader stars, money,...not to say friendships."

SPOTTER Magazine

"Packed with information...there is something here for every Relative Worker."

TNT "Truth News Trends"

"This book grows with the sport. Definitely the bible of RW. I've read and re-read this book in my development in the art."

Jim Winkler, Capt. Ya Who Eight-Way Team

Team Chaos.   *M. Anderson Jenkins.*

ACKNOWLEDGEMENTS

The author would like to acknowledge the many people whose thoughts and ideas have contributed to this book.

The Art of Freefall Relative Work deals with the technique of perfection and the attitude of joy, i.e. flight for the joy of flying. These are esoteric thoughts...subtle in character, difficult to describe, hard to communicate. To produce the clearest statement on the art of skydiving, I embraced all that I had ever heard, experienced or seen relating to perfection and joy.

In formulating my approach to flight for the joy of flying, I used the works of the *Vedas*, the *Upanishads*, Hesse's *Sidhartha*, the books of Carlos Castenada and of Richard Brautigan, the excellent works of W.Y. Evans-Wentz (notably *The Tibetan Book of the Dead* and *The Book of the Great Liberation*), Baba Ram Dass' *Be Here Now* Swami Sri Yukteswar's *The Holy Science*, William James' *Pragmatism*, the writings of Richard Bach, various tests on philisopy, M. Murphy, *Intellectual Digest*, many other people and books too numerous to mention, but especially the Swami Prabhavananda translation of the *Bhagavad-Gita.*

In describing the technique of pefect flight, I am deeply indebted to Jerry Bird, Jim Bohr, Carlos Wallace, Red Kosteba, Stan Troeller, Gruber Gorman, Skratch Garrison, Matt Farmer, B.J. Worth, Rande Deluca, Roger Hull, Kevin Shea, the Greene County jumpers, Ed Fitch, Clyde Jacks, our freefall photographers, and many more. Also, Denis Jenkinson's *The Racing Driver*, Colin Campbell's *The Sports Car: Its Design and Performance*, my yoga teachers, my fencing masters, Pietro Trauffiris' *The Technique of Motor Racing*, and particularly Wolfgang Langewiesch's outstanding text on flying, *Stick and Rudder*, provided excellent technical input.

The real acknowledgement is to my sky-mates on good skydives, teammates from some 15-20 teams, competitors from 16+ years of parachute meets...I acknowledge gratefully and with immense pleasure all the hours of freefall relative work we've shared, and will reshare with those who come later.

Madden Travis "Pat" Works, Jr.

THE ART OF FREEFALL RELATIVE WORK clearly sets forth the techniques of flying. It represents 15 years of experience and four years of research and writing. In vivid detail and in unique original drawings it describes how masterful relative work is done.

Andy Keech

Andy Keech

Ray Cottingham